Praise for

THE VIRTUE OF COLOR-BLINDNESS

"A stirring defense of the principle that you should not gain or lose by the color of your skin. In Professor Archie's book readers will find critical finesse, serious argument, wide-ranging classical elegance, courage, and intelligence."
　　—**Harvey C. Mansfield,** research professor of government, Harvard University, and author of *Machiavelli's Virtue*

"Andre Archie defends the tradition of Frederick Douglass and Martin Luther King and dissects the poisonous justifications for Balkanizing the United States along racial lines."
　　—**Rich Lowry,** editor in chief, *National Review*

"Archie's powerful defense of the once 'liberal' and now 'conservative' ideal of color-blindness is at the same time a warning to liberals and conservatives alike of the profound dangers of identity politics and identitarian ideologies."
　　—**Robert P. George,** McCormick Professor of Jurisprudence, Princeton University, and author of *In Defense of Natural Law*

"An erudite and compelling demolition of today's racialist Left from Derrick Bell to Robin DiAngelo."
　　—**Yoram Hazony,** author of *Conservatism: A Rediscovery*

"Andre Archie is a Thomas Sowell for our generation—a daring scholar whose defense of color-blind principle can't be dismissed as white privilege by even the most race-obsessed critic."
　　—**Daniel McCarthy,** editor, *Modern Age*, and editor-at-large, *American Conservative*

"Andre Archie expertly blends classical philosophy with social and literary analysis in this clarion call for a return to the distinctly American beliefs that inspired such champions of freedom as Frederick Douglass and Martin Luther King Jr."
　　—**Matthew Continetti,** author, *The Right: The Hundred Year War for American Conservatism*

"Andre Archie shows why that clear principle is more than rhetoric: it is an essential truth of American society and its political order."

> —**John Yoo,** Emanuel S. Heller Professor of Law, University of California at Berkeley, visiting fellow, Hoover Institution

"Dr. Martin Luther King Jr. looked forward to the day when all Americans would be judged by the content of their character and not the color of their skin. . . . Now Dr. Andre Archie comes to acquaint another generation of Americans with this tradition, and with its betrayal by some who argue for race-conscious policies. . . ."

> —**Michael Barone,** senior political analyst, *Washington Examiner*, and longtime co-author of *The Almanac of American Politics*

"*The Virtue of Color-Blindness* is the answer to the terrible confusions over race relations in America's schools, universities, boardrooms, and government. Archie brilliantly demolishes the racial hucksters and conflict promoters who are trying to turn back the clock on real American diversity and inclusion."

> —**Christopher DeMuth,** distinguished fellow, Hudson Institute

"Professor Archie points to a path that was not taken, which is black pride in being American felt by members of an intact ethnic and national community. His richly documented arguments provide food for thought on why American blacks did not choose this path."

> —**Paul Gottfried,** Raffensperger Professor Emeritus of Humanities at Elizabethtown College and editor-in-chief of *Chronicles*, author of *The Search for Historical Meaning: Hegel and the Postwar American Right*

"A black man growing up in today's America, Archie combines a rootedness in the Greek and Roman classics with an acute appreciation of the continuing strength of the 'color-blindness' he rightly ascribes to the Constitution, in the spirit of Frederick Douglass's repudiation of the views of the radical abolitionists—views now echoed in the historically illiterate 'woke' invocations of our 'systemic' racism."

> —**Carnes Lord,** Professor of Strategic Leadership at the Naval War College, director, Naval War College Press, and author of *Education and Culture in the Political Thought of Aristotle*

The Virtue of Color-Blindness

The Virtue *of* Color-Blindness

Andre Archie

REGNERY GATEWAY
Washington, D.C.

Regnery Gateway™ is a trademark of Salem Communications Holding
Corporation
Regnery® is a registered trademark and its colophon is a trademark of
Salem Communications Holding Corporation

Cataloging-in-Publication data on file with the Library of Congress

ISBN: 978-1-68451-309-3
eISBN: 978-1-68451-402-1

Published in the United States by
Regnery Gateway, an Imprint of
Regnery Publishing
A Division of Salem Media Group
Washington, D.C.
www.Regnery.com

Manufactured in the United States of America

10 9 8 7 6 5 4 3 2 1

Books are available in quantity for promotional or premium use.
For information on discounts and terms, please visit our website:
www.Regnery.com

This book is dedicated with much love to my
supportive wife, Eleanora Archie, without whom this
and so many other wonderful things in my life would
not have been possible.

Contents

CHAPTER 13
Conclusion: Comfortable Racism

Preface

I truly believe that the United States of America is at a crossroads when it comes to race relations. As a country nearly 245 years old, we have, through fits and starts, navigated issues of race and identity as well as could be expected given the tension brought about by our Founding documents and their principles and the institution of slavery on our shores. Through it all, we've stayed true to the spirit of 1776 and 1863 by recognizing individual rights, not group rights. The American project extols the individual, not the group. This belief was reaffirmed in the Supreme Court's ruling against affirmative action in *Students for Fair Admissions, Inc. v. President and Fellows of Harvard College.* Americans intuitively know it's morally right to judge individuals based on their character and not their race. In other words, Americans know it's morally right to be color-blind.

Recently, however, there has been a weariness when it comes to the issue of race. Due to guilt, Americans seem to have been lulled and intimidated into equating the color-blind approach to race relations to a type of color-blind racism. This is an unfortunate occurrence and portends a dim future for the United States if left unchecked.

Here I sound a call to arms for those conservatives and like-minded Americans who aren't afraid to join me in reclaiming a noble racial tradition: color-blindness! The virtue of this approach lies in the fact that virtue, as Aristotle reminds us, comes through practice and habit. Just as we learn certain skills by performing them—crafts, dance routines, sports, for example—we become morally good by performing actions that embody moral qualities.

Color-blind principles and actions engender natural, sympathetic relations among Americans because they embody the presupposition of a shared American identity that transcends the relatively small differences between us. The conservative case for reclaiming a noble racial tradition of color-blindness, on the other hand, lies in the fact that Americans must "conserve" that which is best, that which is noble, in our history. We must hold firmly to the hard-won gains achieved on the racial front by reminding ourselves of the spirit of 1776 and 1863. And that remembrance begins for me with my family.

Like many other Americans, I was raised in a working-class family that believed in hard work, strong religious values, and a good education. I was taught that middle-class values, as well as an openness towards others, would ultimately pave the way to success. I come from many generations of strivers that believed in perseverance and practiced personal responsibility. Like many other African Americans with a strong, curious mother as the *de facto* head of the family, I was encouraged to appreciate new and different experiences and meet new and different people. My family wasn't naïve about racial discrimination and its insidious effects, but we put discrimination in perspective. Our assumption was that the racist was too conscious of race, not color-blind enough. Worrying about acts of racism wasn't an all-consuming concern for us as it is for many of today's African Americans. Although I mostly grew up among African Americans during my formative years, the positive and open attitude of my family's color-blind outlook carried me to college, graduate school, and to another country to study abroad.

I strongly believe that the moral force of the color-blind approach to race relations must prevail in order for American society to continue to flourish.

To date, no extended attempt makes the conservative case for the virtue of American color-blind principles in a manner that addresses our present turmoil. In fact, I cannot think of any contemporary author on the Left or Right who doesn't think the color-blind approach is at least outdated and probably naïve. So I'd like to offer a much-needed perspective on issues of race, race relations, and ideologies of race.[1]

In light of George Floyd's death, and the subsequent "woke" forces that have swept through American society, such an account is needed now more than ever. These forces have convinced the elites in education and industry to accept uncritically the claim that systemic racism against African Americans infects nearly all aspects of America and its institutions. The false accusation of systemic racism has now been embraced by titans of the tech and financial industries. Establishment political figures on the Right have also endorsed the systemic racism claim espoused by Black Lives Matter. In this caustic environment, it's ironic that color-blindness, a once commonplace approach to race relations, is now considered heresy.

My academic background in ancient Greek philosophy, ethics, and political theory puts me in the unique position to discuss the pernicious racial pedagogies spreading throughout American society in the guise of multiculturalism, the Black Lives Matter movement, and Critical Race Theory (CRT). All of these pedagogies have found fertile ground in the classrooms of our universities, and as an educator on campus, I have a front row seat to their insidious effects. The proponents of these racial pedagogies disdain the ultimate goals of the color-blind approach and wrongly ignore hundreds of years of ethical and religious traditions that reject assigning moral worth to an individual's ascriptive qualities.

Color-blind principles are based on a rich, historical struggle to rise above the natural but base human tendency to be selfish, parochial, and tribal. Humans naturally sort themselves into groups by excluding and marginalizing others. The perverse and obscene instances in history, such as American slavery and the Holocaust, show that such exclusion never leads to anything good. Humans have the intellectual and moral ability to progress beyond tribalism unless we choose to promote perverse institutional and societal incentives. Anti-color-blind pedagogy (and the race consciousness that it cultivates) caters to our base natural tendencies, and it does so in the same manner as all racialist ideologies.

The powerful ideal of color-blindness is more relevant than ever. The virtue of this approach gets at the foundations of many of the arguments about race taking place today in the public square. But it's not simply about race and how Americans discuss it. No, the virtue of color-blindness is at the heart of the American identity. We cannot remain a country without it.

PART I

Giving Accounts:
Reclaiming a Noble Racial Tradition

CHAPTER 1

Introduction

W hen it comes to American race relations, the virtues of the color-blind approach shouldn't be up for debate in the public square.[1] To be color-blind is to understand that an individual's or a group's racial membership should be irrelevant when choices are made or attitudes formed.[2] This approach helps define what it means to be an American in both creed and culture. U.S. Supreme Court Chief Justice John Roberts was giving voice to the American creed about race and racial diversity in his 2007 opinion in *Parents Involved in Community Schools v. Seattle School District* when he argued that "The way to stop discrimination on the basis of race is to stop discriminating on the basis of race."[3] Not judging individuals based on their skin color should be as uncontroversial and intuitive as the statement that "All Men Are Created Equal." Instead, racial color-blindness is controversial, counterintuitive, and considered naïve by the cultural arbiters in the Left-leaning academy, Big Tech, and corporate America.

My intention here is to rehabilitate the noble racial tradition of color-blindness, and to offer a much-needed response to the peddlers of odd, anti-American racial ideas and theories that go against the

American identity. These anti-American ideas and theories are variously known as multiculturalism, "antiracist" pedagogy, diversity, equity, and inclusion (DEI), and Critical Race Theory (CRT). Although my hope is that the arguments I make in defense of color-blindness appeal to the widest possible readership, conservative Americans, due to temperament and justified grievance, are my intended audience.

Some may wonder why I would direct my argument for the color-blind approach at conservative Americans, considering the fact that for nearly half a century they have been unable to neutralize an ascendant, corrosive liberalism. It's no secret that the majority of American institutions that bestow coveted credentials, or grant access to those who have them, have been mostly captured by the Left. Despite conservatism's apparent cultural defeat, I have faith that the right arguments coupled with righteous indignation will position conservative Americans to make up for lost ground in the cultural wars. My book provides both the right arguments and emotional appeal in its defense of color-blind principles.

To defend color-blind principles in these culturally turbulent times, conservatives must first reject an intellectual assumption popularized in the nineteenth century, and now the reigning assumption on most college campuses today. In his book *On Liberty*, British thinker John Stuart Mill argues that truth will emerge if competing ideas are equally entertained in the public square. Otherwise, according to Mill, we would be robbing the human race, if these ideas are right, of the chance to exchange error for truth, and, if they are wrong, of the chance to see more clearly because of the "collision with error."[4] Mill was committed to the belief that human progress is inevitable with the right elites in positions of power.[5]

As a matter of fact, the inevitable triumph of good ideas or truth is *not* guaranteed, and certain ideas should *not* be allowed to gain a foothold in the public square at all. Among those who understand that ideas have consequences, conservatives in particular should be aware of the moral hazard of legitimizing certain ideas by thinking they can be defeated solely by open and rational discussion. One such idea that conservatives failed to challenge and debunk before it took root (in the early 2000s) in influential sectors and institutions of American society is the idea of anti–color blindness. Proponents of anti-color-blind pedagogy believe that the best way to navigate cultural differences in the United States is to openly discuss and highlight racial and ethnic differences. Highlighting differences of race, they argue, makes explicit the structural nature of white economic and social power, and how it is perpetuated at the expense of black Americans and other people of color. Any attempt to downplay ethnic and racial differences, or "homogenize" communities of color by offering platitudes about a supposed "American identity," is seen as a pernicious form of color-blind racism. Contemporary American conservatives failed to see just how corrosive and revolutionary the anti-color-blind pedagogy is. They took it for granted that the idea of color-blindness was a bedrock notion that stood very little chance of being displaced. Given the historical trajectory, legal precedent seemed to affirm conservatives' complacency.

The legal fight against those who opposed the idea that all people are equal before the law was difficult and bloody, but the fight was believed to be just and on the right side of history.

In the 1850s, the Frederick Douglass wing of the abolitionist movement made the case for a color-blind reading of America's Founding documents. That reading led to a split with Garrisonian abolitionists, who agreed with Chief Justice Roger Taney's pro-slavery interpretation of the Constitution. Most important, it was Lincoln's "new birth of freedom" and its attendant Civil War amendments that laid the conceptual groundwork for a color-blind interpretation of America's Founding documents. In 1896, Justice Harlan's dissenting opinion in *Plessy v. Ferguson* eloquently explained the relationship between color-blind principles and the Constitution of the United States:

> But in view of the Constitution, in the eye of the law, there is in this country no superior, dominant, ruling class of citizens. There is no caste here. Our Constitution is color-blind, and neither knows nor tolerates classes among citizens. In respect of civil rights, all citizens are equal before the law. The humblest is the peer of the most powerful. The law regards man as man, and takes no account of his surroundings or of his color when his civil rights as guaranteed by the supreme law of the land are involved.[6]

Nearly five decades later, the civil rights movement was pivotal in laying the groundwork for equal, color-blind protection before the law, ensuring that black Americans not be judged by the color of their skin but rather by the content of their character. Martin Luther King Jr.'s "Letter from a Birmingham Jail" and "I Have a Dream" speech are powerful indictments of segregation and its anti-color-blind position precisely because they appeal to the same Founding American documents and Western philosophical texts that were also used erroneously to support segregation.

This history accounts for conservatives' initial complacency in confronting anti-color-blind pedagogy. In other words, as color-blind principles became enshrined in law, the thinking went, history's movement was believed to be on the side of conservatism.

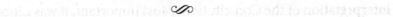

Due to the historical effort in getting America to live up to its color-blind principles, one would think that any attempt to divide Americans along racial and ethnic lines for the sake of fomenting racial grievances would face stiff resistance from most sectors of American society, especially its elites in the academy and corporate America. Unfortunately, this has not been the case. Instead, racial segregation has returned in full, ugly force.

The industry that undermines the idea of color-blindness the most today is the diversity training industry and the many experts it employs to further its goals—usually from within its base located in the academy and corporate boardrooms. Diversity training has become the Trojan horse for far more insidious racial doctrines like Critical Race Theory and "Antiracism." The ease with which diversity training has gained wide institutional support, both on campus and off, has been mind-boggling. The sad fact is, diversity experts have been very successful at promoting racial and ethnic consciousness among their clients.

Diversity training is an outgrowth of anti-color-blind pedagogy. It is intended to make white people aware of their unconscious racism towards people of color and lead them to accept that structural racism against blacks, specifically, is what accounts for the social disparities that afflict these communities. The training makes an emotional appeal to whites to encourage them to think sympathetically about the hard life experiences that communities of color face on a daily basis. The true intention of current diversity training in academic and corporate settings is not to offer a genuine understanding of the "lived experiences" of minorities, and blacks in particular. It is designed to promote intimidation and psychological control over concerned, but racially passive, white Americans.

There is a self-reflective component to diversity training as well. It requires that white Americans see how the lives they live actually work against all people of color in every way possible. For example, if a white person goes to college, gets a degree and a job, and then buys a home in an up-and-coming, affordable neighborhood, he is unwittingly contributing to systemic racism by pushing out people of color who rent in the neighborhood. As this thinking goes, the white person is racist for contributing to gentrification. When the focus on racism is as allusive as "systemic racism" is, it is doubtful that the mandate of the diversity-training experts will ever be achieved. This lack of achievement is good for the experts because it keeps them employed, but bad for society because it stokes racial consciousness and, thus, resentment.

The virtue of color-blindness is that it complements individual responsibility. Martin Luther King Jr. understood the transformative power of personal responsibility and that color-blind principles complement individual responsibility. His successful efforts in fighting racism during the civil rights movement led to changes in the American political system by extending equal access to all Americans, but especially to black Americans and those who had been marginalized historically.

For far too long, American conservatives have been too willing to give a fair hearing to points of view and ideas that are contrary to core American beliefs. In a heterogenous society such as America, very few ideas or points of view have been as destructive as the anti-color-blind pedagogy. However, to highlight the racial and ethnic differences among Americans is to devalue the unifying elements that have traditionally defined the American identity. From coast to coast, civil society has acquiesced to racial practices and policies to such an extent that we now have celebrated authors writing about how babies can be racist. At the elite private school Fieldston in New

York City, the lower school principal recently devised a racial equity curriculum that encouraged children to sort themselves by race so that the white children could become painfully aware of the racism that permeates historically white environments.[7]

The dated social policy of affirmative action is another case in point. Despite the Supreme Court's recent ruling that the policy is unconstitutional, the racial mindset it fostered will take time to uproot. For nearly five-decades, affirmative action has encouraged racial balkanization on the part of blacks and whites. Initially, affirmative action policies were designed to redress the effects of slavery and the subsequent historical injustices against black Americans. The justification for the policies was succinctly stated in President Lyndon B. Johnson's commencement address at Howard University in 1965 prior to his approval later that year of the 1965 Voting Rights Act:

> You do not wipe away the scars of centuries by saying: Now you are free to go were you want, and do as you desire, and choose the leaders you please. You do not take a person who, for years, has been hobbled by chains and liberate him, bring him up to the starting line of a race and then say, "you are free to compete with all the others," and still justly believe that you have been completely fair. Thus it is not enough just to open the gates of opportunity. All citizens must have the ability to walk through those gates.[8]

Specifically, affirmative action was justified on the grounds that African American slavery was unique in American history and, thus, should be acknowledged and atoned for through specific policies that benefit African Americans. All the while, issues of identity continued to grow more fraught. Subsequent to the slavery justification, affirmative action was justified on diversity grounds, which meant all people

of color were incentivized to balkanize along racial lines to gain pref-
erential treatment in school admissions and in employment. It was
Justice Lewis F. Powell Jr.'s 1978 ruling in *Regents v. Bakke* that reorien-
tated affirmative action policies away from redressing the specific
plight of African Americans to the valorization of "diversity" as an
unalloyed social good.[9] Thankfully, the days of affirmative action have
come to an end, which is the reason why the color-blind approach
must prevail. As a country, we can finally do things right. The most
important reason for the need of color-blindness is that it is more
integrative than identities based on the diversity offered by race, gender, or sexual orientation, and more effective at promoting a sense
of American identity. The color-blind approach must become the
reigning *modus vivendi* in America's approach to race relations.

Conservatives should promote, encourage, believe in, and be
willing to go the distance for a color-blind America. Rather than
acquiesce in the face of practices and social policies that balkanize
Americans along racial lines, conservatives should promote the
homogenizing role that faith, family, and tradition have played and
continue to play in the evolution of the country, both politically and
culturally. This can only be done by first recognizing that Americans
should be blind to racial distinctions. African Americans would especially benefit from this homogenizing effort. As one of the oldest
minority groups in America, the black community has already
debated the merits of color-blind principles versus anti-color-blind
pedagogy in the fight for racial equality. The winners of the debate
were the advocates of the color-blind approach to social policy and
the application of law. The culmination of the approach was the social
science brought to bear in the 1954 Supreme Court decision striking

down racial segregation in *Brown v. Board of Education*. It is perhaps understandably difficult for some in the black community to see that real racial advancement has steadily come through color-blind policies, not through intimidating white people. But difficult or not, that is the simple truth.

In a perverse turn of fate, a vocal segment of the African American community and its allies recently have sought to undermine the racial tradition of color-blindness. My goal in *The Virtue of Color-Blindness* is to reacquaint Americans with this tradition and to fight against modern-day segregationists. To turn away from the color-blind approach is to undermine the integrity of individual choices and personal agency. This is replaced by judging others on the basis of their skin color. No good can come from the rejection of color-blindness when it comes to race relations in the United States of America.

CHAPTER 2

Potatoes

C oming of age in Denver during the '70s and '80s in a working-class African American family was an opportune time for me, a restless young boy with aspirations beyond his immediate family and community. Not only was my family encouraging of my ever-changing interests, they also didn't hobble me with a sense of racial grievance when reminding me that African Americans weren't universally popular. Still, American society in general, I believed, was open and welcoming to those, like me, who were willing to explore and contribute something positive to the whole.

The time was optimistic and hopeful. The default position of the leaders in the nation was to accord a degree of respect to different cultures and religions while remaining confident in America's core culture and its traditional values. A sizable number of people were open to genuine interracial interactions and relationships, not the forced multicultural gatherings, affinity groups, and celebrations today that come across as stilted and politically correct. My generation, the X generation, seemed to be the very embodiment of the promise brought about by the sweat and tears of the civil rights movement. Perhaps the openness I sensed and experienced had something to do with the pioneering spirit of the

Mountain West, but whatever it was, I was encouraged to embrace the wider world and its opportunities.

I mainly had a traditional, working class African American experience growing up. We attended church on Sundays, and despite my best efforts to convince anyone who would listen that I was sick and couldn't attend church that day, I ended up like everyone else—in my Sunday best heading off to church to hear Reverend Walker preach way too long. I was a dozer. I often got a nudge from one of my sisters, at the request of my mom, for nodding off while the preacher delivered what seemed like a three-hour sermon. Who could blame me? Three hours on a hard pew listening to parables! We lived mostly around African Americans. My parents divorced shortly after I was born, but my father lived and worked locally. He was a chef at the Denver Press Club. Sadly, it was clear to me at a very young age that my father had priorities other than parenthood. Aside from inconsistent alimony payments, he was not a presence in my life growing up. Lacking a consistent biological father in my home, but positively influenced by my grandfather and sisters, we experienced episodic hardship. Once, we had potatoes for dinner for an entire week because we had very little of anything else edible in our cupboards or fridge. For us it was the opposite of the Irish potato famine. Each night's dinner was a variation on the potato: mashed, boiled, baked, fried, or scalloped. Each of my siblings remembers our potato period slightly differently: one says it was just a few days, the other says it was a day. We all agree, though, that those were trying times. Overall, my mother raised us with a strong sense of personal agency, a cultural trait that was once common in the African American community. For me, my success sequence began with a strong mother, faith and church, respect for elders, and, above all, an appreciation of being born an American. These are the attitudes and values that informed my upbringing, and they are not unique. These are American attitudes and values, values without color or caste. These values are color-blind.

Beyond my family, I was keenly aware of the influence others could have on the development of my sense of self. The African American writer Ralph Ellison refers to this process of influence as "a mysterious enrichment of personality."[1] Despite my loving and supportive family and the heroic efforts of my mom, she couldn't be both a good mother and a good male role model. No matter why my mother found herself in that situation, it was unfortunate. Although I didn't realize it at the time, during high school and college, I sought out those male figures who I recognized could enrich my life in well rounded, intellectually positive ways. I'm not speaking of the type of influence having only to do with the life of the mind, of readings books and discussing ideas. Sure, there was a lot of those sorts of activities. But these male figures seemed to embody what Aristotle refers to in the *Nichomachean Ethics* as the moral and intellectual virtues of practical wisdom, courage, perseverance, and honesty.[2] Two African American men during this period were pivotal in the subsequent direction my life would take: Ken Hamblin and Bill Hervey. I use pivotal deliberately here because, although I didn't know much about either man's personal life, their influence on me within the settings I encountered them, on radio and university respectively, helped guide and hone my budding ambitions.

During my junior year of high school and early college years, Ken Hamblin was a conservative local radio personality and a newspaper columnist in the Denver area. Eventually Ken would achieve national recognition in the 1990s with the syndication of his show, *The Ken Hamblin Show*, and the publication of several books that consisted of collections of his columns and an autobiography. I don't remember how I discovered Ken's radio show in high school, but I remember listening to him for the first time and thinking, *This guy is articulate, smart, black, and very proud to be an American. What a combination!*

I didn't know it at the time, but Ken's parents were first generation Americans from the Caribbean island of Barbados. He was the eldest of five children and raised without a father. Although Ken was of Caribbean descent, he intuitively understood America's color-blind principles and its moral potential, and he understood the African American community. He cared deeply about the community, but was critical of the segment of African Americans that celebrated the culture of poverty through entertainment, especially rap music. As a young listener to Ken's radio program, I remember two themes in particular that resonated with me then, and continue to do so today. The first theme is that Ken thought it was important that African Americans help America better distinguish the minority within the minority in the African American community. The minority within the minority essentially holds African American communities and neighborhoods hostage due to its violent behavior, lack of respect for authority, and high rates of illegitimacy. The burden of making the distinction, Ken argued, should be eagerly assumed by the silent majority of hard-working, decent African Americas who most often feel the effects of crime as well as white backlash. But all too often, hard-working African Americans are shamed into silence by a minority of African Americans when attempting to make the distinction. This minority of African Americans usually benefits from the disfunction it causes and is helped by elite, white liberals who maintain that this "vibrant" minority within the minority is more racially authentic.

The second theme Ken emphasized, often comically, was a variation on the first theme. It was the ham-handed relationship between the disadvantaged segment of the African American community and elite, white liberals. Ken equated this group of white liberals to a fat, lazy dog that sneaks around the henhouse "sucking all the substance out of the freshly laid chicken eggs." His descriptive language was meant to show the debilitating dynamic implied in a type of help offered to disadvantaged African Americans. Help that, at the same time, depletes the motivation and spirit of the disadvantaged by condoning and exploiting its pathologies and fears. The refrain of the white liberal directed at disadvantaged African Americans, Ken would always say, is "blacks are hobbled because America is racist."[3] This is not to say that Ken downplayed the important role white liberals played during the civil rights movement. He did not. His argument is that although African Americans profited greatly from the likes of white liberals such as Michael Schwerner, Andrew Goodman, and Viola Liuzzo during the fight for civil rights in the 1960s, it is now time for African Americans to assume control, as competitive equals, of their own destiny in America.

With a few exceptions, the ideas Ken expressed on his talk radio show about racial matters are, sadly, just as relevant today as they were in the early 1990s. A large segment of African Americans feel like they are hobbled by racism more so today than at any other time in our history. Along with this racial grievance, African Americans have become conscious of race in a way that is completely out of proportion to their actual social status in the real world of the twenty-first century. Ken's honesty and color-blind principles, his show's *raison d'être*, celebrated America, its complexity, and the personal initiative it demands. Race is just one part of that complexity, a tributary within the larger American identity. These are the lessons Ken taught me, and what my family raised me to embrace as I made my way into the wider world.

Bill Hervey was another influential figure in my life. I was introduced to the classics of Western political thought in Bill's Political

Theory Seminar at Colorado State University. He was African American and a Cornell Straussian who had been a student of Werner Dannhauser and Allan Bloom. Political science was Bill's field of study, and he took an interest in my academic development due to my solid grades as an undergraduate in his Western Political Theory course and in his graduate seminar on political theory. Bill loved all things ancient Greek, especially Aristotle and Plato. The sheer mania with which he taught Aristotle's *Politics* and Plato's *Republic* was always accompanied by an equal amount of *sophrosyne*. His teaching and his love of the ancient Greeks were sights to behold. Most important, he taught me that the classical knowledge found mainly in the works of ancient Greek political theory was the very embodiment of a liberal arts education. Such knowledge makes us *free*, he would say, by separating us from particulars of race, of class, of gender, of time and place, and of necessity. Real freedom is intellectual freedom.

Bill imparted to me an appreciation of the beauty and profundity of Western civilization, and the classical world in particular. The 2,500-year-old institution of interlocking ideas, concepts, and procedures was my inheritance just as much it was for any other American citizen. Bill's teaching emphasized the point that we, the citizens of the United States of America, are heirs to the immense intellectual and cultural treasures of ancient Greece and Rome, which creates a *prima facie* case that these two ancient civilizations deserve their privileged position in the West. From the codified curricula of the trivium and quadrivium, to the rigors of philosophy and philosophical expression, to Beethoven, Dave Brubeck, and Miles Davis, to the rule of law, democracy, the city, abolitionism, and property rights, the legacy of the classical world never ceases to amaze.

The testament of those who, like Bill and me, have been seduced by Western culture's siren song, speaks volumes about the power of that legacy, and might be the best way to counter the racially tinged arguments of those who can't see, or refuse to see, that the West's offerings are not intended for a particular racial group, but rather intended for those who are intellectually curious human beings.

Once Bill pointed the way and my own philosophical and cultural explorations started gaining momentum, my admiration for the classical world grew by leaps and bounds, and attests to the powerful appeal of the tradition. My engagement with classical antiquity continues to affirm its civilizing values, rather than the corrosive barbarism of identity politics. As an African American, I am not an immigrant. I can trace my lineage back to slaves (and a few indentured servants) who lived in the early eighteenth century. I am thus living proof that the Classical tradition has just as much to offer the descendant of slaves as it does those who are to the manor born. It goes without saying that these sorts of arguments are not unique to me nor to Bill. African American scholars Frederick Douglass, Booker T. Washington, W. E .B. Du Bois, Zora Neale Hurston, and Ralph Ellison all speak to the West's intellectual tradition as promising a degree of cultural competence and uplift, if one can master it. The veneration of the tradition runs deep and wide. W. E. B. Du Bois confidently says in *The Souls of Black Folk*, "I sit with Shakespeare and he winces not. Across the color line I move arm in arm with Balzac and Dumas, where smiling men and welcoming women glide in gilded halls. . . . I summon Aristotle and Aurelius and what soul I will, and they come all graciously with no scorn nor condescension. So, wed with truth, I dwell above the veil."[4] Ralph Ellison, too, half a century later venerates the literary tradition, all white, that liberated him from a segregated mindset in terms of his potential as a writer. "In Macon County, Alabama, I read Marx, Freud, T. S. Eliot, Pound, Gertrude Stein, and

Hemingway. Books which seldom, if ever, mentioned Negroes were to release me from whatever 'segregated' idea I might have had of my human possibilities."[5] Notice that for both Ellison and Du Bois, contrary to a lot of African Americans in classrooms today, their teachers did not have to "look like them" in order for these two black writers to learn and grow.

Historically, there is no justification for claiming the West's Classical tradition is racist towards people of color. The African American scholar Frank M. Snowden Jr. convincingly argues that classical antiquity was familiar with black people through black-skinned Ethiopians and Nubians, and that neither the Greeks nor the Romans expressed racial animosity toward either. Based on the ancient evidence—literary, epigraphical, papyrological, numismatic, and archaeological—when the Greeks and Romans contrasted the physical characteristics of Ethiopians with whites, the description implied neither physical, mental, nor moral superiority or inferiority on the part of the Ethiopians. According to Snowden, the Greco-Roman world fundamentally rejected color as a criterion for evaluating men, even in the case of slavery:

> Ancient slavery was color-blind. Both whites and blacks were slaves, and the ancient world never developed a concept of the equivalence of slave and black; nor did it create theories to prove that blacks were more suited to slavery than others. Blacks were in a no more disadvantageous position than anyone else unfortunate enough to be captured as a prisoner of war or to be enslaved for whatever reason.[6]

These racialist claims originated with academics at elite institutions in the 1960s and gained momentum in the 1980s with the emergence of multiculturalism. This mindset seeks to highlight the

Afroasiatic roots of the Classics, and, as Victor Davis Hanson and John Heath discuss in their book, *Who Killed Homer?*, sees the West and its classical past as irredeemably racist, imperialistic, and sexist. Reinforced by senior classics professors who, at a minimum, view the ancient Greeks and Romans as merely two ancient cultures among many, the anti-classics mindset has gained enough ground to cause the tradition's defenders to feel as if they're fighting a rear-guard battle. And that's a shame, because whatever a student's skin color or ethnic background, the Classical tradition itself still has a power to challenge and change minds that the Afroasiatic alternatives can't match. This, along with many other enduring lessons, is what Bill taught me.

CHAPTER 3

What Is the Color-Blind Approach to Race Relations?

When Martin Luther King Jr. spoke in 1963 during his March on Washington, he famously said in his "I Have a Dream Speech" that he dreamed that his "four children [would] one day live in a nation where they would not be judged by the color of their skin but by the content of their character."[1] Earlier that same year, and in a radically different context, King's "Letter from a Birmingham Jail" spoke searingly about the collateral damage of racial prejudice done to black Americans and white Americans and done to "those great wells of democracy which were dug deep by the founding fathers in their formulation of the Constitution and the Declaration of Independence."[2] No other public figure in modern times has expressed sentiments so resonant with the color-blind tradition in the Western intellectual tradition. Given King's moral and practical advocacy, he seems to have understood that he was a mere vessel of many strands of ethical thought that privilege individual character (*êthos*), and its concomitant choices and actions, over conventional and arbitrary markers of distinction such as a person's sex or race. Many of those strands of ethical thought inform my own approach to relations between all Americans, especially the relations between America's two oldest groups, the white and black communities.[3]

My approach to race relations, the color-blind approach, is grounded on the moral belief that the mere possession of hereditary qualities, like race, should not confer moral merit by their possession or nonpossession. Instead, moral merit can be, and should be, conferred upon an individual's actions, because actions reveal one's character. When I speak about character, I should be understood as speaking about the right desires, feelings, pleasures, and pains that make up the states of the virtuous character. The belief in character, as opposed to ascriptive qualities, as the locus of moral agency has a rich and comprehensive history in the West, and it continues to animate our own Founding documents and way of life. In order to see just how significant prioritizing character over ascriptive qualities has been in the West, we must begin with the' some of the first recorded reflections on the moral importance of character, which begin with the ancient Greek ethical tradition knowns as eudaimonism. As an ethical framework, initiated by Plato and Aristotle, eudaimonism assumes that the ultimate human good is happiness, and the task of ethics is to figure out what exactly happiness is and what contributes to happiness.[4] Unlike modern ethics, like Utilitarianism or versions of deontology, which require criteria for selecting the best action, ethics for the ancient Greeks is concerned with the best way to live; it is person-centered rather than act-centered. The best way to understand the differences between ancient and modern ethics is to see how modern ethic's emphasis on "criteria" for action can be justified in ascribing moral status to ascriptive qualities. As a moral theory, Utilitarianism can be complex, but for the sake of showing the difference between ancient Greek ethics and modern ethics, I'll briefly focus on the most basic aspects of Utilitarianism.[5]

The most salient Utilitarian criterion is the one that is applied to actions to determine whether or not those actions are morally permissible. The criterion is the utility principle. Utilitarians must ask the question, "Will this particular action produce greater overall human well-being?" The question seeks to assess the morality of an action by whether the action itself produces the most utility, or at least as much utility, as any other action. Utility, defined as pleasure or happiness, resides either in actions pertaining to intellectual pursuits or the satisfaction of bodily desires. The utility question is successfully answered, according to Utilitarians, once additional criteria are satisfied. These additional criteria include the requirement that actions be guided by the quantity of utility of the audience of one's intended actions or actions being assessed. It is with this criterion that Utilitarianism and, by extension, the modern approach to ethics, is susceptible to attributing moral status to ascriptive qualities like race. The vulnerability of Utilitarianism to this kind of interpretation, and the modern, rule-based approach to ethics in general, resides in its lack of a comprehensive criteria-standard for determining the nature and limits of the criterion that go into evaluating actions. What's to prevent race or racial characteristics from being used as a criterion in deciding whether or not an action produces the greatest amount of utility, happiness, or well-being? Real-world examples of race or racial characteristics being used in the service of promoting utility through public policy are the various percent plans that are designed to admit to selective state universities the top ten percent of graduating students from high schools within a state. The Texas Top Ten Percent Plan is probably the most well-known among the percent plans. The assumption of the percent plans is that because most high schools, especially in urban areas, are segregated along the lines of class and race, the top performing graduating high school students guarantee that at least a percentage of a flagship university's incoming cohort of students will be of color and/or economically disadvantaged. It's mostly issues of race, and the underrepresentation of African Americans at flagship universities, that have fueled the popularity of these race conscious programs. But these programs are very blunt and crude instruments of utilitarian social policy that end up "type casting" schools based mostly on the ascriptive quality of race.[6] In arguing for these types of percent programs, it's not enough for state legislators to say that they are merely using segregated schools as a proxy for socio-economic factors like poverty. Race itself becomes the means by which moral merit is conferred on the individual or group, rather than on the individual's character, or personhood, as expressed through his freely chosen actions. Going forward, these proxy maneuvers will be one of the ways institutions indirectly promote racial goals and confer racial spoils while at the same time formally rejecting race conscious policies.

Ancient Greek ethics, on the other hand, is person-centered, which means that in thinking about the best way to live or what to do, the ancient Greeks focused on two things: determining the right thing to do and doing it properly, motivated by one's virtuous character. Although bad people can certainly do good actions, they cannot do actions as the good person would do them, which is to say, properly motivated. Properly motivated actions are anchored in and generated by one's virtuous character, which is the end result of an individual's autonomous choices. Character is not the product of factors that fall outside of the sphere of choice, voluntary action, and how choice is exercised morally.[7] The body and what belongs to it are not involved with the manifestation of virtue. Thus, for the ancient Greeks, ascriptive qualities like race played no role in the formation of character nor the assessment of character.

The virtuous character comes about by habit or practice; virtue is a disposition that an individual manifests through the motivation to act in an appropriate way and to the appropriate extent in the right circumstances. Habit, and the development of habits, is crucial for moral education, the formation of character, and most crucially, for moral motivation. In the same way that we learn arts or sports by doing them, so we become morally good by performing morally good actions. Doing courageous deeds makes us courageous persons. The person having the virtue, courage, tends to do courageous kinds of actions courageously. Virtue is a way to secure both the orientation towards the right things to do but also the doing of them through the proper motivation. In short, the ancient Greeks, most notably Plato and Aristotle, relied on the formation of character to secure good actions properly motivated.

A passage in Plato's dialogue *Apology* is a good illustration of the emphasis the ancient Greeks placed on character, as opposed to ascriptive qualities like race. The context of the conversation in the dialogue is cautionary and ironic because Socrates is defending himself during his trial. He is being accused of a number of different things, one of which is the claim that he corrupts the youth. In the passage, Socrates admonishes the Athenians for prioritizing conventional and bodily goods over the good of the soul, namely, a virtuous character.

> Then, if one of you disputes this and says he does care [about wisdom, truth, and virtue], I shall not let him go at once or leave him, but I shall question him, examine him and test him, and if I do not think he has attained the goodness that he says he has, I shall reproach him because he attaches little importance to the most important things and greater importance to inferior things. I shall treat in this way anyone I happen to meet, young and old, citizen and stranger, and more so the citizens because you are

more kindred to me. Be sure that this is what the god orders me to do, and I think there is no Greater blessing for the city than my service to the god. For I go around doing nothing but persuading both young and old among you not to care for your body or your wealth in preference to or as strongly as for the best possible state of your soul [one's virtuous character].[8]

The emphasis here is the contrast between appearing to care for the proper type of goods, and actually caring for those goods as expressed through one's commitments and, by extension, virtuous character. The "most important things" Socrates speaks of are those things that fall outside the body and what belongs to it. These things are truth, wisdom, and virtue, and they enable one to properly use the body and what belongs to it, as well as external goods (money, friends, and so forth). Ascriptive qualities, like race, fall into the class of things that pertain to the body and what belongs to it. In a modern context, another way of stating Socrates' overall point is to say that the content of one's character determines one's attitude towards the body and what belongs to it, like race, and external goods like money and friendships. This brings me back to the color-blind sentiments of Martin Luther King Jr.[9] He tapped into the rich Western philosophical tradition initiated by the ancient Greeks to gain much needed support from a broad swath of Americans who knew that racism was wrong. Socrates' message that character counts resonated with the deep sense of dignity had among good, decent Americans.

Aristotle is the other foundational figure in the person-centered, *eudaimonistic* concept. Whereas Plato's *Apology* focuses on the role of virtue in the proper use and perspective toward the ascriptive qualities of the body and what belongs to it, Aristotle's *Nicomachean Ethics* illustrates the role choice plays in the conferring of moral merit upon human action. Here too, like Plato, Aristotle argues that the type of choices one makes is anchored in one's character, certainly not in the body and its physical qualities. There is a world of moral difference, for example, between a mercenary soldier fighting courageously to protect a foreign land versus a home-grown patriot fighting courageously to protect his own country's land. The patriot's actions exhibit the proper type of courage in the appropriate circumstances, properly motivated. Accordingly, moral merit can be conferred upon the patriot's type of courage. The mercenary's actions do not exhibit true courage at all, because his apparent courage is perverted by ulterior motives that prevent the proper type of courageous motivation. Aristotle's comments on the importance of choice, voluntary action, as a reflection of character state:

> Still they [the ignorant] themselves by their slack lives are responsible for becoming men of that kind, and men are themselves responsible for being unjust or self-indulgent, in that they cheat or spend their time in drinking bouts and the like; for it is activities exercised on particular objects that make the corresponding character. This is plain from the case of people training for any contest or action; they practice the activity the whole time. Now not to know that it is from the exercise of activities on particular objects that states of character are produced is the mark of a thoroughly senseless person. Again, it is irrational to suppose that a man who acts unjustly does not wish to be unjust or a man who acts self-indulgently to be self-indulgent. But if without being ignorant a man does

the things which will make him unjust, he will be unjust voluntarily.[10]

Character can be morally praised or condemned because it results from our prior choices and actions, and our prior choices and actions were voluntary, so we are responsible for our own characters in the present. It makes no sense to praise, condemn, or assign moral status to ascriptive qualities like race because one's race is an indelible feature of one's body, and it has not come about through choice. When society does assign moral status to race, as Dr. King illustrates, bitterness and hatred become the main currency through which Americans interact with one another. The reason for the antipathy has everything to do with the arbitrariness of assigning moral status to racial characteristics. When character becomes the main currency through which Americans interact with one another, the relations between the races are less stilted, more fluid, and natural. Fairplay and judging others by the content of their character is an abiding theme in the intellectual traditions of Western thought.

These ancient Greek sentiments regarding personhood and character go well beyond Plato's and Aristotle's writings. The theme of character extends from the Romans to early Christianity to the English and American abolitionists who opposed slavery.

The Roman philosopher and Stoic, Cicero, discusses the significance of character quite movingly in his influential dialogue *On Friendship* (*De Amicitia*). The conversation is mainly conducted by Gaius Laelius, along with several other minor participants. The topic of the dialogue is the question, how should one handle the death of a good friend? Laelius's friend, Africanus, has recently died. The philosophical thrust of the piece is an exposition of friendship and death from the Stoic point of view. The essay is filled with many insightful points, but the small section of the essay that emphasizes character in the manner that I have been discussing will be my main focus. Cicero juxtaposes the permanent things we should value in relationships with the superficial things that have an appeal to our conventional notions of success. Cicero frames the issue as follows:

> For what is so ridiculous as to take delight in a host of unsubstantial things, such as honor, glory, a house, the clothing and care of the body, and not to take as much delight in a living soul endowed with virtue—a soul that has the power to love, or—so to speak—to return love? .... But if we add this further point—and we shall be quite right in so doing—that there is nothing that so attracts and draws anything to itself as likeness of character does friendship.... [11]

Here we see in Cicero's comments on the body and character the continuing thread that runs through the West's ethical traditions: the soul-body distinction. In this distinction, the virtuous soul, most important, represents character and is the ethical anchor for the body and what belongs to it. One's body and what belongs to it—conventional goods—can only be put to good use by a good character. Friendship, according to Cicero, is the ideal relationship to see character played out through voluntary, reciprocal action. Therefore, ascriptive qualities, like racial characteristics, play no substantial role in relationships, especially friendships. And in a multiracial society like the United States, citizens who are genuinely friendly towards one another tend to be color-blind.

The history of Christianity and its ethical traditions has done a great deal in the West to promote an aspirational transcendence beyond ascriptive qualities. Even though the language used to describe the soul's relationship with the body started shifting around the thirteenth century from a singular soul animating a single physical body to a communal spirit (*spiritus*) the individual is initiated into, the intention is consistent with the ethical discourse on character expressed by the ancient Greeks. The one ironic difference between the two traditions, however, is that Christianity initiates the individual into a supra-ascriptive realm. That is, Christianity, like other ancient religious traditions, called on its believers to renounce their worldly ascriptive qualities and embrace a more singular, universal, Christ-like character. All worldly ascriptive qualities would, in relation to the Christ-like character, cease to be of significance. Paul's epistles, in Galatians and Corinthians, express this universal, Christ-like character: "There is neither Jew nor Greek, there is neither slave nor free, there is no male and female, for you are all one in Christ Jesus" (Galatians 3:28 ESV); "For in one spirit we were all baptized into one body—Jews or Greeks, slaves or free—and all were made to drink of one Spirit" (1 Corinthians 12:13 ESV).

The belief that the color-blind principles of character and its voluntary actions are the rightful place to assign moral merit—as opposed to assigning moral merit to ascriptive qualities like race that are non-voluntary, or to brute qualities of one's body, period—has played a significant role in the various liberation movements in the West. Keep in mind here that I am not referring to the lawless twentieth century National Liberation Movements (NLMs) that perpetually menace third world countries.[12] I am referring to liberation movements like the English and American abolitionists who opposed the institution of slavery on constitutional and philosophical grounds. One such figure who was profoundly influenced by the West's tradition of color-blind principles and the sentiments of liberty that grow out of those principles is Frederick Douglass.

That influence, in the form of a relatively short book titled *The Columbian Orator*, came to Douglass at a time in his life that proved pivotal and long-lasting. The impact of *The Columbian Orator* on Douglass' emotional and intellectual development speaks to the powerful influence of the Western philosophical tradition's embrace of character and its appeal to the innate intellectual curiosity of all human beings—from the humblest slave to the most high-toned aristocrat. Douglass was a thirteen-year-old slave boy in 1830 when he first bought a copy of *The Columbian Orator*. As he tells it in *My Bondage and My Freedom*, he was intrigued and motivated to buy the book after hearing a group of little boys who said they were going to "learn some little pieces out of it" for an upcoming exhibition. What he discovered in *The Columbian Orator* was a collection of eighty-four moralistic and literary entries, spanning prose, plays, and speeches designed to promote elocution and character, and to educate school children in the ways of American republicanism. For our purposes, it is significant to point out that Douglass does not complain about the absence of writers of color in *The Columbian Orator*. He is not seeking racial validation so much as he is seeking the free exercise of his intellectual and physical capacity through the written and spoken words chronicled in the book. Douglass is seeking liberty! He says as much when commenting on the lessons he took from *The Columbian Orator*:

> The dialogue and the speeches were all redolent of the
> principles of liberty, and poured floods of light on the
> nature and character of slavery. With a book of this kind

in my hand, my own human nature, and the facts of my experience, to help me, I was equal to a contest with religious advocates of slavery, whether among the whites or among the colored people, for blindness, in this matter, is not confined to the former.[13]

Douglass speaks movingly here of two animating ideas that are essential to the tradition of color-blindness: human nature is ultimately rational (it's the differentia of the human species) and liberty is an inherently moral good. Despite the servitude he finds himself in, Douglass's capacity as a rational human being puts him on an equal moral footing with any white person and equips him with a righteous indignation towards his fellow religious African Americans who insist that slavery should be endured with humility for spiritual reasons. It also frees him from the physical and spatial limitations that is slavery. Not in a literal sense, but in the sense that his new awareness helps him to appreciate that his servitude is merely by convention, not by nature. The selections Douglass encountered in *The Columbian Orator* resonated powerfully within him because they portrayed the best examples of what human nature can produce on an intellectual level.

Douglass also speaks of *The Columbian Orator* as "redolent of the principles of liberty." In speaking of liberty, he argues that slavery, in all of its aspects, is opposed to republicanism. The idea he is expressing is that the individual, no less the slave, is free to exercise his birthright of agency for the development of his own personhood and for the development of a community that's consistent with liberty. Both of these ideas are illustrated in an especially poignant dialogue from *The Columbian Orator*. In *My Bondage and My Freedom*, Douglass identifies the exchange between a recently recaptured slave and his master as one that he "perused and reperused with unflagging satisfaction." The dialogue between the master and the slave commences after the slave, for the second time, failed to escape his bondage. The master admonishes the slave for his ingratitude because he has accorded the slave some material comforts not given to the other slaves. In answering the charge of ingratitude, the slave and master have the following exchange:

> Slave. I am a slave. That is answer enough.
>
> Mast. I am not content with that answer. I thought I discerned in you some token of mind superior to your condition. I treated you accordingly. You have been comfortably fed and lodged, not over worked, and attended with the most care when you were sick. And is this the return?
>
> Slave. Since you condescend to talk with me, as man to man, I will reply. What have you done, what can you do for me, that will compensate for the liberty which you have taken away?
>
> Mast. I did not take it away. You were a slave when I fairly purchased you.
>
> Slave. Did I give my consent to the purchase?
>
> Mast. You had no consent to give. You had already lost the right of disposing yourself.
>
> Slave. I had lost the power, but how the right? I was treacherously kidnapped in my own country, when following an honest occupation. I was put in chains sold, sold to one of your countrymen, carried by force on board his ship, brought hither, and exposed to sale like a beast in the market, where you bought me. What step in all this progress of violence and injustice can give a right? Was it in the villain who stole me, in the slave-merchant who tempted

him to do so, or in you who encouraged the slave merchant
to bring his cargo of human cattle to cultivate your lands?[14]

It's no wonder that Douglass was transfixed by the slave's piercing
words. They foreshadow both the words and deeds for which
Douglass gained his much-deserved influence in American history
as a champion of liberty and as a proponent of color-blind principles.
As I've shown, liberty, color-blind principles, and character are not
unique to the nineteenth century and Douglass's milieu. As an
American, an African American, he inherited longstanding moral
and ethical traditions three thousand years in the making. It's these
traditions that Martin Luther King Jr., too, harnessed to inspire and
change a nation in the twentieth century. We must remember, however, that these uniquely Western moral and ethical traditions have
not been without their detractors, black and white; they've been
fiercely contested by various forces over the centuries. The opposition
to the early civil rights movement was clear for all to see. In the case
of Douglass, little is known of his battle with fellow abolitionists over
his decidedly color-blind approach to interpreting Founding American
documents like the Constitution of the United States and the
Declaration of Independence.

CHAPTER 4

Frederick Douglass and the Abolitionists: The Anti-Slavery, Color-Blind Constitution

From certain quarters recently, we loudly hear the accusation that racism in America today is systemic. The idea conveyed by the charge is that people of color, especially African Americans, face the headwinds of discrimination in every sector of American life. While we know that making such an argument in twenty-first century America is unfounded by the facts, in the nineteenth century, discrimination against African Americans was factually systemic. Once slavery was legally abolished, emancipation and reconstruction promised very little in the face of organized violence, political and economic marginalization, and segregation that blacks experienced. But even under these trying circumstances, Frederick Douglass insisted on a color-blind approach to interpreting Founding American documents like the Constitution. The reason for his insistence is a story worth telling.

Frederick Douglass, who had recently escaped from slavery, came into contact with the powerful anti-slavery words expressed by William Lloyd Garrison in 1839 in his abolitionist paper the *Liberator*. As Douglass puts it in *My Bondage and My Freedom*, Garrison's "paper took its place with me next to the bible."[1] The *Liberator* was an

35

anti-slavery publication established in 1831 and founded by Garrison. The publication's mission was twofold: to agitate for the abolishment of slavery and, just as significantly, to challenge the legitimacy of Founding documents like the United States Constitution that served to perpetuate the institution of slavery and its anti-color-blind principles.

The eventual split, then, between Douglass and Garrison over competing claims about the extent to which the Constitution and other Founding documents are instruments of slavery boils down to Garrison believing that the Founding documents are anti-black through and through, and Douglass believing that they could be interpreted as abolitionist instruments, color-blind instruments, through and through. Of course, Douglass evolved intellectually over the years to embrace an anti-slavery, color-blind reading of American Founding documents. Douglass seems to have grasped the idea that these two approaches to interpreting the Founding documents were mutually entailing. That is, if the Constitution were an anti-slavery document, it also had to be a color-blind document because blacks were synonymous with slavery in the United States of America.

Douglass's Constitutional Transformation

What made the split between Douglass and Garrison so fierce, besides the paternal relationship Douglass had with Garrison, were the extreme, uncompromising philosophical positions Garrison took toward human nature, politics, natural law, and government in general. Garrison and the Garrisonians often portrayed the Constitution as a pact or covenant with death and hell because they believed it was a pro-slavery document. Characteristic of these strong sentiments are the following pronouncements:

> There stands the bloody [fugitive slave] clause in the Constitution—you cannot fret the seal off the bond. The fault is in allowing such a Constitution to live an hour. . . . When I look on these crowded thousands and see them trample on their consciences and the rights of their fellow men at the bidding of a piece of parchment, I say, my curse be on the Constitution of these United States![2]

And in an address that demanded northern Christians cease to associate with pro-slavery Christian congregations in the south, Garrison's reading of Isaiah 28:14–18, "took on secular connotations"[3]:

> Because ye have said, we have made a covenant with death, and with hell are we at agreement . . . your covenant with death shall be disannulled, and your agreement with hell shall not stand; when the overflowing scourge shall pass through, then ye shall be trodden down by it.[4]

Garrison's constitutional beliefs were, fundamentally, informed by his acceptance of perfectionism. His perfectionism was motivated by two assumptions. One assumption is that man is capable of freeing himself from the inclinations of human nature, and the other is that through will and faith, man can achieve perfection on earth. What follows from the assumptions is that all earthly institutions are essentially corrupt by the mere fact that they acquiesce to man's corrupt nature. Whereas, if man would obey Christ, there would be no need for status hierarchies among people. In other words, "When men had become perfect, all, including females and blacks, would coexist as equals. The distinction of rank, place, and function that set one man above others in the church or state would be swept away."[5] Given that human institutions stifle the realization of human perfection, a nonresistant pacifism is the only course of action in the political sphere, according to Garrison. Nonresistant pacifism renounces government, voting, and holding political offices.

Ultimately, Garrison's perfectionism and nonresistant pacifism put him in the uncompromising position of believing that the only way to abolish any form of unequal treatment by an individual or group toward another—be it in the form of collecting taxes, military command, or slaveholding—requires a universal moral emancipation. That is, any emancipation short "of our whole race from the dominion of man, . . . and bringing them under the dominion of God, the control of an inward spirit, the government of the law of love, and into the obedience and liberty of Christ" would be wholly deficient in bringing about lasting antislavery political change.[6] As one can imagine, Garrison's strident beliefs put him at odds with his fellow abolitionists. Mockingly, his political pacifism was referred to by his opponents as the "no-human-government" stance.[7] To demand that there must first be universal moral regeneration of all men before effective anti-slavery political engagement could take place was an irrelevant diversion from the exigencies of the moment, Garrison's critics argued. As a consequence of Garrison's perfectionism and nonresistant pacifism, three philosophical positions guided him and the Garrisonians in general.

The first position promoted a positivist jurisprudence. The Garrisonians held that law, in contrast to natural law, was simply what judicial tribunals, government, and the people have defined it to be. That is, law is a "rule of civil conduct prescribed by the Supreme power of a state, commanding what its subjects are to do, and prohibiting what they are to forbear."[8] Even if civil, municipal, or national law get expressed contrary to what is considered just or natural law, as in the case of the justification of slavery, the dictates of a positivist jurisprudence require that the jurist apply the law as a representative of civil government. When it comes to law, the Garrisonians ask, who determines what is just and right? Their jurisprudence answered that "for the purpose of the civil government of any nation, the majority of that nation is to decide, and their decision is final, and constitutes, for that nation, Law."[9] Ironically, the Garrisonian position on law, and the interpretation of law, had a stifling effect on the extent to which extra-constitutional principles could be brought to bear on constitutional matters, especially as they relate to the relationship between civil law, natural law, and slavery. As the legal historian William M. Wiecek puts it:

> Under positivist assumptions, men were doomed to accept
> the law as they found it, with all its deformity, and aboli-
> tionists were precluded from working for change through
> and with extant law and legal systems. The Garrisonians'
> postulates locked them into a legal status quo that could
> be changed only by a millennial and universal shift in pub-
> lic sentiment. In this way, as in others, Garrisonian theory
> led functionally to de facto conservatism.[10]

That conservatism, the status quo, was clearly on the side of those, like John C. Calhoun, who argued that the American Founding documents, especially the Constitution, precluded any sort of color-blind reading of the document.[11]

The second position, resulting from the implications of the first, was that, given the Garrisonians reinterpretation of the *Somerset* case, which left the institution of slavery unencumbered due to colonial customs, the Constitution was deemed a pro-slavery document. The case was important to the Garrisonians, and it would become increasingly important to Douglass in his embrace of the Constitution as an anti-slavery document. The *Somerset* case ruled that Charles Stewart couldn't lawfully transport James Somerset out of England, an African slave purchased in Virginia, who had been taken to England by Stewart. At issue was the reach of Lord Chief Justice Mansfield's decree:

> *The state of slavery is of such a nature, that it is incapable of being introduced on any reasons, moral or political; but only positive law, which preserves its force long after the reasons, occasion, and time itself from whence it was created, is erased from memory: it's so odious, that nothing can be suffered to support it but positive law. Whatever inconveniences, therefore, may follow from a decision, I cannot say this case is allowed or approved by the law of England; and therefore the black must be discharged.*[12]

The Garrisonians construed the case as only applying to England, and as statutory law codifying customary practices. Thus, slavery existed as a custom "as ratified by legislative enactments of the colonial assemblies. . . . The laws of the provincial and state legislatures and the new state constitutions continued slavery intact."[13] On these grounds, the Garrisonians justified their position of non-allegiance and sectional disunion.

The third position argued that slavery was a state issue, so there was no constitutional mechanism introduced by the Continental Congress "that framed the Declaration of Independence nor [was] the Confederation Congress that drew up the Articles . . . empowered by the states to meddle with their internal social institutions. . . . Black slaves were the exception to the Declaration."[14] Thus, the Garrisonians' reading of the Constitution argues that:

> our fathers were intent on securing liberty to themselves, without being very scrupulous as the to the means they

used to accomplish their purpose. . . . [T]hough they recognized occasionally the brotherhood of the human race,
in practice they continually denied it. They did not blush
to enslave a portion of their fellow man . . . while they were
. . . boasting of their regard for the rights of man.[15]

On the basis of Garrison's steadfast commitment to specific
beliefs that informed his brand of abolitionism—perfectionism, nonresistant pacifism, positivist jurisprudence—his split with Douglass
hinged.

Having been affiliated with the Garrisonian abolitionists prior to
his split with Garrison, Douglass embraced some of the nonresistant
pacificist positions championed by the group. Douglass's main position prior to the years leading up to his decisive break with the
Garrisonians was that any type of political action or endorsement of
the anti-black, pro-slavery Constitution of the United States was a
moral abomination. Political inaction and moral condemnation was
the appropriate attitude to take toward such a pro-slavery document.
On these grounds, the whole apparatus of the American government
was corrupt and in need of universal moral emancipation, just as the
human race as a whole was in such a need. For Douglass's goal, black
emancipation, not until the Constitution was "made consistent in its
details with the noble purposes avowed in its preamble" could it be
made color-blind.[16] After much reflection, a lot of reading, and having extensive conversations with leading figures of the abolitionist
movement who argued that the Constitution was anti-slavery,
Douglass, starting in the winter of 1851, ceased to endorse the idea
that the Constitution of the United States was pro-slavery. In contrast
to the Garrisonians, Douglass was intent on showing just how important the Preamble to the United States Constitution was in the fight
for emancipation, and for a color-blind reading of the document.

> We the people of the United States, in order to form a more
> perfect Union, establish Justice, insure domestic Tranquility,
> provide for the common defense, promote the general
> Welfare, and secure the Blessings of Liberty to ourselves and
> our Posterity . . .

The Preamble Is Framed for Freedom

Douglass's considered conclusion was that every section, every clause, of the Constitution should be read in light of its Preamble. Reading the document in this way renders it an anti-slavery document and makes it incumbent upon the federal government to work for slavery's abolishment. Douglass had his misgivings about construing the Constitution according to the strict rules of interpretation advocated by abolitionist jurists. Their interpretation of the Constitution was legalistic and literal, all for the purpose of avoiding reading the document in light of the intention of the framers, which were pro-slavery intentions. But there was one nagging question that Douglass couldn't quite rid himself of about the framer's intentions: "Is it good morality to take advantage of a legal flaw and put a meaning upon a legal instrument the opposite of what we have good reason to believe was the intention of the men who framed it?"[17] Ultimately, these misgivings gave way to the practical necessity of reading the Constitution as a color-blind document. To have the Constitution on the side of the abolitionist cause was a moral and legal boon. The Garrisonians, on the other hand, were hamstrung. They couldn't appeal to anything, other than their moral indignation, that would speak to the conscience of a Christian people. As it stood, the Garrisonian position on the Constitution cast all Americans, Northerners and Southerners, as participants in a wicked country. Douglass understood that he needed allies in the fight for emancipation, and that allies are hard to come by without an appeal to those symbols that elicit a love of country. Douglass claimed the Constitution for himself and his cause.

In the spring of 1851, Douglass finally went public with his changed views on the Constitution. As he declares in the editorial, "Change of Opinion Announced," in the *North Star*, May 15, 1851, his change in opinion on the subject of slavery and the Constitution wasn't a hasty change. The writings of some of the leading abolitionists and jurists of the day—Gerrit Smith, Lysander Spooner, William Goodell—had brought him to his "present conclusion."[18] There were other jurists who influenced Douglass's thinking too. The abolitionist Salmon P. Chase was very helpful as well in shaping Douglass's views on reading the Constitution as an anti-slavery document. Who were these men? And in what ways did their constitutional beliefs and interpretations become weapons in Douglass's fight for an anti-slavery, color-blind Constitution? These men were white Americans who came from old, Northern, distinguished families. With the exception of abolitionist Gerrit Smith, they weren't particularly wealthy, but they were all committed to promoting the equality of the races through a color-blind reading of the American Constitution. Their racial advocacy and intellectual focus on behalf of helping black Americans achieve equality before the law were quite remarkable. It's doubtful that the Frederick Douglass we revere so much today would have achieved the status he presently occupies without having been shaped by the ideas he inherited from these men.

The one philosophical assumption that seems to have united these abolitionists and jurists who influenced Douglass so much is their commitment to natural law. Blackstone's discussion of the "law of nature" figured prominently in each of their writings on the role of natural law and slavery.[19] They argued that, unlike positive law, the law of nature is unhistorical. It exists objectively both as a norm for individuals, communities, and the state, and as a limiting principle in the political arena where objective right could be repudiated by the legislator. All positive laws are valid only insofar as they derive from natural law, which is the source of an individual's natural rights—life, liberty, property—and the duty of government to protect. Their position on natural law also informed their belief that common law contained the spirit of natural law. Their interpretation was that common law limited the state's power to endorse slavery, and it was the *Somerset* case that ruled definitively on the relationship between common law and slavery. Accordingly, the abolitionists and jurists Douglass was influenced by held that *Somerset* showed that common law was inconsistent with slavery, and that certain legal procedures like trial by jury and habeas corpus protected an individual's liberty.

Gerrit Smith, the abolitionist from New York, was instrumental in Douglass's eventual acceptance of the Constitution as an anti-slavery document. Smith's anti-slavery advocacy was mainly in the form of delivering speeches, letters, personal correspondences, and funding Douglass's abolitionist projects. Smith was persistent in proselytizing for the belief that the Constitution was anti-slavery through and through, and that it only needed to be read and applied in a way that expedited the "overthrow of the whole system of American slavery."[20] It was the abolitionists' duty, according to Smith, to wield the weapon of constitutionalism, because "To give up the Constitution is to give up the slave."[21] William Goodell, too, influenced Douglass through his abolitionist journalism. His compendium of radical abolitionist perspectives on the Constitution, *Views of American Constitutional Law*, was one of the key texts that helped him see that the Constitution should be "wielded in behalf of emancipation."[22]

Whereas Goodell and Smith's abolitionist work centered on their journalistic contribution to black emancipation, the Massachusetts-born Lysander Spooner equipped Douglass with an interpretive lens through which the Constitution can be read as a protector of individual liberty and a liberator of the enslaved.

Legal theorist Lysander Spooner focused his efforts on expounding a close, textual reading of the Constitution to show that it's an anti-slavery document. He lays out his approach in his book *The Unconstitutionality of Slavery*. The aim of Spooner's book is to show, first and foremost, that constitutional legitimacy and natural rights are coupled. A constitution's legitimacy derives from its power to protect natural rights. "In order that the contract of government may be valid and lawful, it must purport to authorize nothing inconsistent with natural justice, and men's natural rights. It cannot lawfully authorize the government to destroy or take from men their natural rights. . . ."[23] The institution of slavery, the vilest type of destruction of man's natural rights, delegitimizes any government that condones such practices. Another concern addressed in Spooner's book is to show that the promoters of a pro-slavery Constitution, abolitionists and pro-slavery advocates alike, have read more into the Constitution than what's actually there. They go "behind" the letter of the Constitution to discover its meaning in history, practice, and intentions. Alternatively, a close textual reading of the document, aside from the natural law argument, reveals that the Constitution is anti-slavery. Given that the Preamble of the Constitution explicitly states its purpose, which is to "secure the Blessings of Liberty to ourselves and our Posterity," Spooner argues that the Constitution must be "explicit, distinct and unequivocal" in its pro-slavery stance. Spooner's intellectual justification for his approach, an approach Douglass was very much receptive to, was first expressed by Chief Justice John Marshall in the 1805 U.S. Supreme Court ruling in *United*

States v. Fisher. The case centered on bankruptcy, and whether it was constitutional to prioritize one class of creditors over another. Marshall's landmark opinion was decisive for abolitionist interpreters of the Constitution like Spooner. Marshall argued, "Where rights are infringed, where fundamental principles are overthrown, where the general system of the law is departed from, the legislative intention must be expressed with irresistible clearness, to induce a court of justice to suppose a design to affect such objects."[24] In short, when words are ambiguous or simply unclear, and can be interpreted in line with natural rights or in opposition to natural rights, the interpretation consistent with natural rights is *the* meaning that should be given to the words under consideration. Based on these Anglo-American interpretive rules and strictures, Spooner justified his anti-slavery, pro-color-blind reading of the Constitution.[25]

Salmon P. Chase was another influential figure in Douglass's move away from the Garrisonian position on the Constitution and slavery. Chase was born in New Hampshire in 1808, but eventually moved to Ohio to practice law. He was at first slow to embrace the abolitionist cause, but once he did, he became a fierce proponent of both an anti-slavery politics and an abolitionist jurisprudence. Unlike Garrison and his fellow travelers, Chase saw practical politics as one of the only effective ways to exercise political action in opposing slavery. Chase held two political beliefs that especially appealed to Douglass. The first belief was that slavery perverted the idea of labor. Slavery pitted slave labor against free labor, and in so doing, it perverted government from carrying out its intended purpose: to protect individual liberty. The second belief was that the institution of slavery was strictly local, but had transgressed beyond its bounds. This transgression posed a mortal threat to Republican government. Chase argued that, outside of the states that legislated in support of slavery, the institution of slavery shouldn't receive a national sanction. This "freedom national" argument was used by Chase, for example, to oppose the 1850 Fugitive Slave Act on the grounds that the Federal government has the power to outlaw slavery in all Federal territories.[26] Chase says as much in an 1856 letter to a fellow abolitionist named Theodore Parker. To Parker he confides that: "The General Government has the power to prohibit slavery everywhere outside of Slave States. . . . I say, then, take the conceded proposition and make it practical. Make it a living reality! Then you have taken a great first step. Slavery is denationalized."[27]

Chase's arguments and political action did bear fruit for the abolitionist cause over the subsequent years. The 1856 and 1860 Republican platform borrowed from his constitutional arguments against slavery. Additionally, during the early years of the Civil War, Chase served as the Secretary of the Treasury under the Lincoln administration. And in 1864, Lincoln appointed Chase to the U.S. Supreme Court, replacing Chief Justice Roger Taney.[28]

The evolution of Douglass's views on the American Founding documents, especially the Constitution, is quite remarkable. As a former slave, Douglass recognized the instruments of power that upheld the institution of slavery. The most formidable instrument that kept the slave and slavery intact was ignorance. In the beginning chapters of *My Bondage and My Freedom*, Douglass apologizes to the reader for not knowing the details nor the precise time of his birth and knowledge of his parents. As he puts it, "Genealogical trees do not flourish among slaves. . . . [Slavery] is a successful method of obliterating from the mind and heart of the slave, all just ideals of the sacredness of the family, as an institution."[29] In addition to the slave's familial ignorance, Douglass recognized that slavery shrouded the constitutional birthright of the American slave; it encouraged political and constitutional estrangement on the part of black Americans. The fundamental question that seemed to have motivated Douglass's intellectual evolution away from the Garrisonian abolitionists was: "Is the slave a political orphan in the United States of America?" The Garrisonian answer was "yes." Douglass' answer was "no." As I've shown, and what Douglass expresses explicitly, he was tired of arguing on the side of the slaveholders. But that was precisely what Douglass was doing in siding with the Garrisonians in believing that the Constitution was an anti-black, pro-slavery document. Calhoun and his allies vehemently believed, too, that blacks were not entitled to citizenship nor·could the Federal government outlaw slavery in the states.

Natural Law and the Constitution

For Douglass, the culmination of the influences of Gerrit Smith, Lysander Spooner, William Goodell, and Salmon P. Chase resulted in an approach to interpreting the Constitution and the Declaration of Independence that was honest and prescient. Douglass's interpretation was honest because he recognized that the aspirational, color-blind Constitution was different from the American government. The two are not identical. As Douglass puts it in his 1860 address, "The Constitution of the United States: Is It Pro-Slavery or Anti-Slavery?", in Glasgow, Scotland, to confuse the American government with the Constitution is to see the "ship as identical to the compass. The one may point right and the other steer wrong. . . . The Constitution may be right, the Government wrong."[30] The fact that government may be governed by people who are corrupt and wicked doesn't mean that the Constitution is wicked and corrupt. The distinction Douglass is making runs throughout his various speeches and writings during this period. Douglass was committed to the belief that the spirit of the American Founding documents as expressed in the Declaration of Independence and the Preamble to the Constitution must be read in light of the *letter* of each of these documents. The all-important question isn't whether slavery existed at the time the Constitution was adopted, or whether the American courts acquiesced to pro-slavery interpretations of the Constitution. The question is, according to Douglass in the Scotland address, "Does the United States Constitution guarantee to any class or description of people in that country the right to enslave, or hold as property, any other class or description of people in that country?" Douglass answers a resounding "no." In answering no, he takes the interpretive fight to his opponents who argue that the Constitution is a pro-slavery document. Douglass does this by first analyzing several provisions of the Constitution that were used both by pro-slavery advocates and the Garrisonians, and then he concludes his address by speaking about the Constitution's natural law principles as a rebuke to those who wish to interpret the document and its provisions as supporting slavery. As he says, "These are the provisions which have been pressed into the service of the human fleshmongers of America."[31] I'll focus on a just few of those provisions as representative of the strict constructionist approach Douglass applied to the Constitution. The provisions are Article I, section 2 (the three-fifths clause); Article I, section 9 (the twenty-year interval on abolishing the importing of slaves into the United States); and Article IV, section 2 (the fugitive slave clause).

Regarding Article I, section 2, Douglass, for the sake of argument, proposes a counterfactual. He says let's assume the provision "refers" to slaves (although he says it could just as easily apply to aliens living in the United States, those who have not been naturalized).[32] But assuming the less charitable reading of the provision, Douglass argues that the provision is still to the disadvantage of the slave states because it takes from those states two-fifths of their natural basis of political power. In short, Douglass interprets the provision in terms of political power. He rejects the idea that the Constitution endorses

the belief that the black man is three-fifths of a white man. He concludes his analysis of the provision by arguing that "A black man in
a free state is worth just two-fifths more than a black man in a slave
State, as a basis of political power under the Constitution. Therefore,
instead of encouraging slavery, the Constitution encourages freedom
by giving an increase of 'two-fifths' of political power to free over
slave States. So much for the three-fifths clause; taking it at its worst,
it still leans to freedom, not to slavery."[33]

　　Douglass's interpretation of Article I, section 9 (the twenty-year
interval on abolishing the importing of slaves into the United States)
begins by stating that because the American government couldn't
ban the slave trade, assuming the clause was even referring to the
African salve trade, for twenty years, American Statesman [Founders]
were not perpetuating and protecting slavery, but rather "in providing for the abolition of the slave trade, thought they were providing
for the abolition of slavery."[34] Even the British abolitionists like
Wilberforce and Clarkson, Douglass argues, took the view that was
in line with the Founders' view: to abolish the slave trade is to abolish
slavery in due course. But even if the provision is taken to refer to
the African slave trade, Douglass concludes his analysis by pointing
out that, in effect, the Constitution is anti-slavery because it is telling
the slave states that if they are admitted into the American Union,
"the price you will pay" is that the trading in slaves will be put to an
end, and that the provision "showed that the intentions of the framers
of the Constitution were good, not bad."

　　Douglass's discussion of Article IV, section 2 (the fugitive slave
clause) shows just how significant the thought of Smith, Spooner,
Goodell, and Chase was on him. He begins by recounting a false
version of how the fugitive slave clause was debated and then adopted
by the Founders. The version that he recounts drips with sarcasm
and derision. That pro-slavery version tells a story in which two

South Carolinian delegates to the ratifying convention, Pierce Butler
and George Pickney, "moved that the Constitution should require
that fugitive slaves and servants should be delivered up like criminals,
and after a discussion on the subject, the clause . . . was adopted."[35]
The provision was also adopted, according to this version, by various
other states during their ratification of the Constitution. In fact,
Douglass says, the true version of the origin of the provision was that
once it was introduced and discussed, the two delegates were told
that the Constitution should not admit any language endorsing the
idea that that there can be property in man, nor should it mention
the word "servitude." And so, the word servitude was struck from the
provision. "But it may be asked," Douglass continues rhetorically, if
this clause does not apply to slaves, to whom does it apply? He
answers that when the provision was adopted it applied namely to
indentured servants. Those who had come to America from around
the world "and had, for a consideration duly paid, become bound to
'serve and labour' for the parties to whom their service and labour
was due." These were contractual relationships, which the slave was
not, and could not, be a party to: "The legal condition of the slave
puts him beyond the operation of the provision." Here we see
Douglass reflecting on the methodological approach applied to
Article IV, section 2—an approach he learned from Spooner, and
clearly on display in his justification for construing the constitutional
provision as he does in his address. He says that "in all matters where
laws are taught to be made the means of oppression, cruelty, and
wickedness, I am for strict construction."[36] Echoing the words of
Blackstone and Chief Justice Marshall, Douglass's strict construction
in interpreting the Constitution demands that whenever rights are
subject to curtailment, liberty is minimized, or the ambiguity of language is determinative in denying rights altogether, either the provision under consideration has to be expressed as an explicit

curtailment with "irresistible clearness," or the law "must be construed strictly in favour" of justice and the principles of liberty.

Douglass's closing remarks highlight the point that any interpretation of the Constitution must be done in the context of its Preamble,
and the Declaration of Independence and its natural right principles.
There we find the clearly stated purpose for which the document was
framed and adopted. The stated purpose prescribed in the Preamble
includes: "union, defence, welfare, tranquility, justice, and liberty." In
none of the six purposes mentioned, Douglass argues, is slavery mentioned. It's not mentioned because slavery is opposed to each of the six.
Neither does the "We" in the Preamble refer exclusively to white people. Why would the supposed friends of the Negro, Douglass won-
ders, deny anything guaranteed under the Constitution to the
Negro unless the document, in plain and common English, says
otherwise? The document is explicit in its declaration that "no person
shall be deprived of life, liberty, or property without due process law."
There are other guarantees the Negro is entitled to under the
Constitution. Douglass mentions trial by jury, the writ of habeas
corpus, and that it "secures to every state a republican form of government." He concludes the address by making it clear that there is
certainly a price to pay for tolerating the institution of slavery among
a divided people. "Slavery is essentially barbarous in its character,"
he says. It is opposed to civilization, and where it is allowed to fester,
where it "meets no reproving frowns, and hears no condemning
voices," barbarism flourishes. Therefore the "bond" of the states, "the
Union," must work to bring the slave states under the purview of the
free states. Subsequently, in keeping with the principles of the
American Founding, Douglass, in an explicit rejection of the
Garrisonians' nonresistant pacifism, says that he had now grown
toward "reform, not revolution. I would act for the abolition of slavery through Government—not over its ruins."

As I have mentioned, the honesty of Douglass's approach to interpreting the Founding American documents resides in his thesis that the plain, common sense reading of the Constitution renders it anti-slavery and, by extension, color-blind. This reading ultimately led to the split between Douglass and Garrison, but Douglass recognized that the tools for the eventual dismantling of slavery, like the Constitution, were his birthright just as much as they were for Garrison. The issue, then, boiled down to the question: "How should the tools be used?" With the help of Gerrit Smith, Lysander Spooner, William Goodell, and Salmon P. Chase, we know how Douglass answered the question. Approaching the Constitution in the way that he did also shows an uncanny prescience on the part of Douglass. He anticipates many of the themes, debates, and conflicts that have shadowed America's steady, consistent progress on racial matters. Yes, progress. Most conservatives recognize this fact. It has been much harder for liberals to understand that, for right-thinking African Americans, what America is and what it stands for has never been the issue: the issue has been to get America to stand by the principles expressed in the Declaration of Independence, the Preamble to the Constitution, and the Constitution itself. America isn't perfect, but where we are in the twenty-first century, it has *mostly* succeeded in practicing what it preaches on racial matters, and that's progress. In so many respects, Douglass anticipates many of the color-blind themes Martin Luther King championed. In the true sense of the word, Douglass was a patriot.

There's no doubt that Douglass's association with Garrison and the Garrisonians was impactful. Douglass tells us as much in his writings and speeches. But Douglass also reminds African Americans in particular, at least for those who can listen, that we need to be careful about other people's plans to alleviate our *supposed* racial predicament in America. We, as a community, need to conserve all that's best in us, and within the American tradition, for the sake of our own racial uplift. The journalist and social critic George S. Schuyler captures Douglass's sentiment when he says: "He [the black American] has been the outstanding example of American conservatism: adjustable, resourceful, adaptable, patient, restrained. . . . This has been the despair of the reformers who have tried to lead him up on the mountain and who have promised him eternal salvation. Had he taken the advice of the minority of firebrands in his midst, he would have risked extermination."[37] Well said!

PART II

Opponents of Color-Blind Principles

CHAPTER 5

Working the System: Sophistry

The color-blind approach to race relations is being challenged by those who insist that racism is a systemic feature of American society, and Western civilization in particular. The systemic racism claim has also been referred to as the "original sin" argument. The argument holds that America's racism against people of color isn't simply a fading anachronistic holdover from a bygone age, but that racism's presence permeates every aspect of America because it flows from the very foundations of the American Founding. Hence, it is a secular form of original sin.

The anti-color-blind defenders are an assorted group of individuals. These individuals populate and influence the institutions and organizations that hold an enormous amount of moral sway over everyday Americans. They consist of primary and secondary school teachers, journalists, public intellectuals, activists, and academics. It's no accident that these individuals find themselves in positions of power among their like-minded cohort. Any attempt to undermine a society's traditional beliefs and practices requires, as the Italian Marxist Antonio Gramsci puts it, a concerted long march through a society's leading cultural institutions. In the context of race relations, the long march began with the institutionalization of African American studies departments in the 1960s. Besides some of the nuttiness that was initially taught in these programs, a narrative of separateness has been their consistent refrain from the very beginning: *The United States and its history is irredeemably racist and exploitative. Slavery is America's original sin.*[1] The proper way to construe the institutionalization of the African American studies regime, and its departmental descendants today, is to make an important distinction between the "core" and "fringe." America was settled by an English-speaking Protestant core, the attributes of which include both substantive ideas such as constitutionalism, rule of law, human equality, and local traditions among particular communities found throughout early America. These attributes became the pillars on which America waged a revolutionary war against England and African Americans fought their enslavement and second-class citizenship in America. The fringe elements, on the other hand, are not necessarily characterized by race, ethnic origin, or religion. They are characterized by a mindset; a deep disdain of many of the institutions and values that have defined America for nearly three hundred years, including academic merit, the bourgeois values of delayed gratification and, most important, marriage. This mindset is captured by the word *oikophobia*, a topic I'll address in chapter 10.

African American studies departments, and ethnic studies departments as a whole, have played an influential role both in academia and in undermining an American identity that is grounded in color-blind principles and transcends race. Firmly ensconced in the ivory tower, these anti-color-blind defenders have parleyed their dubious moral authority into aiding and abetting a cottage industry of the aggrieved. Some of the most pernicious and delusionally aggrieved of these individuals have been academics and public intellectuals who claim to be speaking racial truth to power. It's precisely because they are articulate and clever that they have an audience, influence, and a following, but also the reason why they must be dealt with harshly. They must be called out and challenged. As Socrates reminds us in commenting on his treatment of the poets like Homer in Plato's *Republic*:

> It isn't that they aren't poetic and pleasing to the majority of hearers but that, the more poetic they are, the less they should be heard.[2]

Ideally, the less we hear from these anti-color-blind academics and intellectuals, the better. Assuming that these individuals will not go quietly into the night, it's incumbent upon those who have an abiding love of America, imperfect though she might be, to defend America and the color-blind traditions that we all cherish. The specific academics and intellectuals that have most effectively challenged the color-blind position in the public square are, in order of influence, Derrick Bell, Ta-Nehisi Coates, Ibram X. Kendi, and Robin DiAngelo. With the exception of Bell, the remaining three are living, contemporary authors whose books and public appearances continue to command an inordinate amount of public attention with the help of their well-placed allies in the legacy media. This is especially the case for Ta-Nehisi's 2015 autobiography, *Between the World and Me*. But there would be very little of importance in Coates's writings on race without having been influenced by the writings of Derrick Bell.

CHAPTER 6

Derrick Bell

"Isn't there a parallel, Professor, between the formalists' reactionary faith in their supposedly apolitical principles and the modern captivation with color-blind neutrality?"[1]

Derrick Bell

The name often associated with the term Critical Race Theory (CRT), and the movement it has spawned, is Derrick Bell (1930–2011). He has been described as the "intellectual father figure" and "Godfather" of the movement that emerged in the 1980s, having itself emerged from a broader intellectual movement in the 1960s called critical legal studies.[2] Both movements were marginal, academic preoccupations that had a smattering of advocates. It wasn't until the death of George Floyd in Minneapolis that Critical Race Theory, in particular, emerged from the university classroom to exert an antagonistic, racial influence on policies of mainstream institutions and discussions in the public square.

To say that Critical Race Theory is diametrically opposed to the tradition of color-blindness is an understatement. The movement makes a mockery of everything America stands for, and its ideas continue to wreak havoc on America's fabric by incessantly appealing to our worst racial fears about one another.

Two of the most harmful ideas that critical race theorists hold are that "racism is ordinary, not aberrational," and that racism will never be eradicated in America because it serves the material and psychic interests of both white elites and working-class whites.[3] Given these ideas, Bell completely rejects the assumption that African American interests are served by traditional legal standards of objectivity and neutrality. Instead, the only way to advance African American interest in an environment of systemic racism is to use law to practice positive discrimination. That is, law should be politically motivated, results oriented, and anti-color blind. But even this type of positive discrimination is not enough. The only way that African Americans can truly advance in America, despite their best efforts, is if white America sees its interest as also advancing at the same time. This power dynamic is referred to by Bell as Interest Convergence, which is the thesis that the "majority group [white Americans] tolerates advances for racial justice only when it suits its interest to do so."[4] Bell construes some of the most important legal rulings during the civil rights movement from the racialist perspective of the convergence thesis. He does this, for example, with the 1954 Supreme Court ruling striking down separate but equal in *Brown v. Board of Education of Topeka*. Whereas the ruling is broadly considered one of the landmark cases in the fight for color-blind equality, and rightfully so, Bell's interpretation of the decision is that it should be understood in the context of white supremacy:

> The decision in *Brown* to break with the Court's long-held position on these issues cannot be understood without some consideration of the decision's value to whites, not simply

those concerned about the immorality of racial inequality, but also those whites in policymaking positions able to see the economic and political advances at home and abroad that would follow abandonment of segregation.[5]

Through the lens of the convergence thesis, Bell's interpretation of *Brown* argues that the case was decided the way it was as a marginal acknowledgement to its black citizens that they are equal before the law, but mostly the *Brown* decision was a gift to white self-interest both at home and abroad. Some of those economic and political self-interest concerns include shoring up America's credibility in its struggle against communism. Domestically, the ruling served white self-interest, according to Bell, by functioning as a ruse of sorts that kept blacks, and other people of color, committed to the political process, its ideals of freedom and equality, and committed to hope. Bell's Interest Convergence perspective on *Brown* is part and parcel of a broader assumption that critical race theorists take quite seriously. This assumption is that institutions, law in particular, create illegitimate social and cultural hierarchies that result in the subordination of whites over blacks and other people of color. Institutions are able to mask their practice and perpetuation of racial subordination by obscuring, obfuscating, their motives through an apparent "impartial" and "neutral" type language.

Not only must African Americans accept that racism is the default position towards them in everyday interactions with their fellow white Americans, they must also accept that they lack the agency to advance their own interests. Both claims are counter to the history that I recount of Douglass and the abolitionists in chapter 4. The abolitionist movement alone is a counter narrative to Bell's Interest Convergence thesis and its assumption that African Americans lack agency to improve their own well-being in America. But, then again, Bell has no interest in historical facts, nor is he interested in racial fraternity.

In some ways, it is surprising that Bell and his work have come to symbolize a movement that threatens to unravel so much of the progress on race that America has undergone. Born in Pittsburgh to a working class Presbyterian family, Bell was the first in his family to go to college. He received a law degree, worked in the Civil Rights Division of the Eisenhower Justice Department, then worked for the NAACP's Legal Defense Fund, and eventually became Harvard Law School's first black tenured professor in 1971. From most firsthand accounts I've read and the recorded media events of his that I've watched or listened to, Bell was a rather mild-mannered man. Or, more accurately, he was a wolf in sheep's clothing. His seemingly conventional professional and academic career belied deep racial animus toward white people, toward African Americans who saw racial matters differently from his own views, and toward America and what it represents. The basic proposition around which Bell's writings revolve, and the one that his acolytes work relentlessly to contrast with another basic proposition, "All Men Are Created Equal," is the claim that:

> Black people will never gain full equality in this [America] country. Even those herculean efforts we hail as successful will produce no more than temporary "peaks of progress" short-lived victories that slide into irrelevance as racial patterns adapt in ways that maintain white dominance. This is a hard-to-accept fact that all history verifies. We must

acknowledge it, not as a sign of submission, but as an act of ultimate defiance.[6]

This sort of racial pessimism and defeatism informs all of Bell's writings on race. As if to give his ideas on race a gloss of profundity, he relates the plight of African Americans with the mythical Greek hero Sisyphus, as told by the existentialist writer Albert Camus. The Greek hero was condemned for all eternity to rolling a rock up a mountain, watching it roll down, and rolling it back up. We must take pride in Sisyphus's defiance, even in the face of defeat. Bell sees the burden of being black in America as equivalent to Sisyphus's rock, so even in the face of white racism and unending racial sub-ordination, he argues that we are supposed to take pride in black defiance. This is all intellectual nonsense, and it should be seen as such by any decent and relatively informed American. It is a conun-drum, however, why Bell has managed to become the pied piper of an anti-American, anti-color-blind movement that has gained broad institutional access at all levels in contemporary America. His status isn't due to an in-depth empirical analysis of the persistence of rac-ism. Nor is it due to a sustained, in-depth treatment of a racial matter that has proved to be insightful and constructive. His status seems to reside mainly in his appeal to a marginal, fringy element both within the academy and in the broader American society. In the academy, the least rigorous departments, but the most aggrieved, think Bell has something worthwhile to contribute to the classroom. They find his legal storytelling profound, compelling, and defiant. His writing also provides these academics a safe space in an environ-ment in which they often feel alienated. Outside of the university, those who take Bell's racialist pronouncements seriously are a fifth column of sorts, an enemy within American society, who are happy whenever they are working to undermine the national interest. Just as troubling, perhaps even more so, are those who go along with Bell's ideas simply to get along. This latter group can best be described as useful idiots.

Bell and CRT take great pride in their defiant mode of fighting an alleged systemic racism by presenting truth in new forms by provoking resistance, and "confounding those committed to accepted measures for determining the quality and validity of statements made and conclusions reached. . . ."[7] These new forms are especially provocative when the innovators are from historically marginalized groups, and especially offensive to the historically privileged group (white males) who sit in judgement of them. The new forms include storytelling, short stories, personal anecdotes, and narrative analysis. In other words, as one of his fictional characters says in his short story "A Law Professor's Protest," "I truly believe that analysis . . . through fiction, personal experience, and the stories of people on the bottom illustrates how racism continues to dominate our society. . . . In fact, a good deal of the writing in critical race theory stresses that oppressions are neither neatly divorceable from one another nor emendable to strict categorization."[8]

The fictional character in this passage sums up succinctly the reason for the poor quality that's often on display in Bell's writing, especially in his collection of parables and short stories, *Faces at the Bottom of the Well*. The subjective and preachy nature of Bell's stories make any sort of analysis of his work a pointless endeavor. Based on most of Bell's fictional writing, and nearly all of the other writings that make up CRT, the latter claim in the quoted passage above that "oppressions" tend to be inseparable and resistant to easy categorization isn't quite true. Flip to any page in *Faces at the Bottom of the Well*, and you'll read that whites are the oppressors and blacks are the victims. So, the more accurate claim should be, for people of color, oppression by whites is an expression of white supremacy, pure and simple, and white supremacy is ubiquitous and exercised in countless ways. Bell's racial sentiments expressed here are merely the tip of the iceberg. For no other group in America, except for white Americans, would we tolerate the wholesale racial demonization of a group.

Bell attempts to provoke racial awareness in his readers, but African American are portrayed as too dumb to recognize that they'll always be under the thumb of white people. In Bell's allegory, "Racism's Secret Bonding," data storms of information about the effects of racism on African Americans are relayed directly to the minds of white people of the United States. Not only do they receive data about the vast inequality that exists between blacks and whites, whites actually *feel* the misery that characterizes the racial oppression blacks have to endure daily. Of course, whites cannot and will not tolerate the racial data storms, so they use their enormous power to get the government to stop them. The moral of the story is that heretofore the African American community and its civil rights leaders held the belief that through education white Americans would become more sympathetic and, thus, would push for reforms that would solve the race problem. However, no such reform was ever forthcoming because, as the story's characters explain, whites benefit from racism:

> "You know . . . education leads to enlightenment. Enlightenment opens the way to empathy. Empathy fore- shadows reform. In other words, that whites—once given true understanding of the evils of discrimination. Once

able to feel how it harms blacks—would find it easy, or easier to give up racism."

"Yes, that is certainly what we have hoped for . . . but now you doubts? Doubts based on—"

"Experience . . . experience. Oh, they [white Americans] may not know the details of the harm [racism], or its scope, but they *know*. Knowing is the key to racism's greatest value to individual whites and to their interest in maintaining the status quo."[9]

For white readers of Bell, there seem to be only two types of provocations that get elicited by these sorts of passages: white guilt or deep resentment towards African Americans. Honestly, any white person who reads Bell or any other CRT advocate, other than to vehemently refute their claims, is seriously misguided. It would seem that the awareness he intends to provoke among his African American readers, given the hopelessness of their situation that he portrays, is the nihilistic, racial reckoning we continue to witness in the assaults against Asian Americans and other groups perpetrated by African Americans.

Bell's stories hardly succeed in their purpose because the topic of race and racism can only be discussed so much. For Bell, racism is ubiquitous; it's in every nook and cranny of American society. His reductionist approach to race rings hollow. The main reason for the hollowness is that there's very little in his stories, and how they're presented, that appeal to a non-racial, American esprit de corps of shared values and communal norms. There are no values and procedures from which racial matters can be viewed: sympathy, comparison, and argument. In short, Bell is opposed to any notion of color-blind principles or procedures around which real issues of racism and its effects can be discussed. The reader of Bell's work is left with no objective metrics or point of reference to make sense of what he and CRT claim about the lack of progress and the persistence of racism in America.

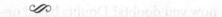

When considering the real-world consequences of a racist ideology masquerading as a more muscular civil rights movement, the inevitable question that arises is, "What is to be done with CRT?"[10] The inevitable answer to this question for conservatives is to ban Critical Race Theory without further ado. Several states have passed anti-CRT legislation, but the results have been mixed. Educators are shocked by such legislation, both on the Right and the Left. In university classrooms the assumption is that even controversial theories like CRT should get a fair hearing, and to argue otherwise is considered fascist. As I mentioned in the introduction, some conservatives are blindly committed to John Stuart Mill's principle that truth will emerge if competing ideas—like CRT versus color-blindness—are equally entertained in the public square. "Truth will emerge" in the American context should be understood as ideas consistent with the proposition that "All Men Are Created Equal." Unfortunately, the ideas that reign victorious in the public square today are decidedly opposed to color-blindness. So much for competition among ideas. Those conservatives who understand that ideas have consequences, the moral hazard of legitimizing certain ideas, like CRT, by thinking they can be defeated solely by open, abstract, and rational discussion, account for the racial quagmire we presently find ourselves in as a society.[11]

American conservatives should always keep in mind that the formation of an American national identity requires that certain extreme, anti-American theories and ideas that are presently given free rein in the public square (especially on college campuses) be marginalized. Of course, I am speaking mainly of CRT here, but I could just as easily insert DEI, antiracism, wokeism, and multiculturalism. Each of these racialized ways of thinking, and the corrosive identity politics they have unleashed, has proved to be a powerful counter-narrative to the traditional American sentiment *e pluribus unum*. The public square is now dominated by competing racial narratives, all enjoying equal billing. Eventually these competing narratives will come into conflict. Co-existence among diverse groups can be maintained only through a color-blind national identity grounded in a robust common narrative. Curtailing the most radical anti-American voices in the public square would be one way of dealing with racist counter narratives. Accordingly, a moderate amount of illiberalism directed at the expression of certain types of speech might be necessary. The "systemic racism" and "white privilege" tropes are the types of speech I have in mind. Institutional practices of illiberalism to curtail political extremism are not unprecedented within our constitutional framework. The Supreme Court, for example, consisting of nine unelected justices with life tenure, and the Senate, in which a collection of members who represent a small fraction of the country can block legislation, are examples of illiberal checks and balances within our constitutional framework that are in defense of democratic constitutionalism. Likewise, within the public square, a moderate illiberalism should be brought to bear on CRT and its racist intellectual offshoots, in defense of America and its color-blind principles.

CHAPTER 7

Ta-Nehisi Coates

"'White America' is a syndicate arrayed to protect its exclusive power to dominate and control our [black bodies]. Sometimes this power is direct (lynching), and sometimes it is insidious (redlining)."[1]

Ta-Nehisi Coates

D espite the fact that *Between the World and Me* is clearly anti-white, and profoundly anti-American, David Brooks' July 2015 *New York Times* opinion column, "Listening to Ta-Nehisi Coates While White," gushes about the education Coates's book has provided the public. Written as a letter to Coates, Brooks' piece opens with the following remarks:

> Your new book, "Between the World and Me," is a great and searing contribution to this public education [in the context of the killings in Ferguson, Baltimore, and Charleston]. It is a mind-altering account of the black male experience. Every conscientious American should read it.[2]

Quite the praise from Brooks, even though Coates goes on to disparage the first responders who died during 9/11 as racist, as "menaces of nature."[3] In general, Coates opposes everything that Frederick Douglass and subsequent generations of African Americans stood for. In the face of overwhelming odds, African Americans have understood the importance of character, and not judging others based on skin color.

Brooks is an intelligent observer, so what accounts for his praise for such a blatantly racist book and its author? Brooks' endorsement, may have carried a degree of authority given the eventual sales of the book. Perhaps a deep dive into its anti-color-blind arguments will provide some perspective as to its appeal to people like Brooks. Recall the combative exchange that took place in 1963 between the black writer Ralph Ellison and literary critic and *Dissent* editor Irving Howe. Ellison takes Howe, and white liberals in general, to task for believing that black Americans' racial predicament is so forlorn that the only path for the authentically black intellectual is to protest and agitate constantly. Commenting on the negative effects of such myopic beliefs, Ellison suggests that there is not much difference between a white liberal and a segregationist:

> Irving Howe would designate the role which Negro writers are to play more rigidly than any Southern politician—and for the best of reasons. We must express "black" anger and "clenched militancy"; most of all we should not become too interested in the problems of the art of literature, even though it is through these that we seek our individual identities. And between writing well and being ideologically militant, we must choose militancy.[4]

Coates's argument is an updated version of Irving Howe's argument, so much so that it seems a call for a return to segregation. As for the choice between writing well and over-the-top name-calling ideological militancy, Coates and his liberal supporters like Brooks prefer the thrill of militancy.

Between the World and Me falls within the exhortative tradition of black American letter writing, which means Coates consciously modeled his essay on James Baldwin's *The Fire Next Time*. Baldwin's letter best exemplifies the exhortative tradition's attempt at practical persuasion and advice-giving on the topic of race and race relations. Whereas Baldwin's letter is addressed to his black nephew, Coates's letter is addressed to his fifteen-year-old black son. The overall message behind Coates's letter is the depressing and debilitating belief that the racial circumstances he was born into nearly four decades ago are mostly the same today, and have been inherited by his son. Accordingly, the advice he gives his son in the letter is supposed to be of obvious utility. His introductory remarks capture the sentiment:

> The destroyers [white people] are merely men enforcing the whims of our country, correctly interpreting its heritage and legacy. It is hard to face this. But all our phrasing—race relations, racial chasm, racial justice, racial profiling, white privilege, even white supremacy—serves to obscure that racism is a visceral experience, that it dislodges brains, blocks airways, rips muscle, extracts organs, cracks bones, breaks teeth. You must never look away from this. You must always remember that the sociology, the history, the economics, the graphs, the charts, the regressions all land, with great violence, upon the body.[5]

Here we see Coates's tendency to exaggerate for literary effect. This tendency characterizes his entire essay. The son of a Black

Panther father and schoolteacher mother, a self-reflective Coates explains to his son that when he was fifteen, he and all the other black people he knew in Baltimore "were powerfully, adamantly, dangerously afraid." The fear manifested itself in the surly bravado that is often associated with ghetto culture—"rings and medallions," playing the dozens, "puffy coats," oversized "T-shirts," rap music, and ritualized but violent street fighting. In the beatings he got from his father and the beatings his grandmother got from her father and the beatings administered by black mothers to save their girls from drugs and drug dealers, "guns, fists, knives, crack, rape, and disease," fear was the culprit. Even in Philadelphia, where Coates's extended family lived, fear was pervasive among his relatives. He accounts for the fear by explaining to his son that it stems from a "nakedness," a vulnerability before the elements of the world:

> The nakedness is not an error, nor pathology. The nakedness is the correct and intended result of policy, the predictable upshot of people forced for centuries to live under fear. The law did not protect us. And now, in your time, the law has become an excuse for stopping and frisking you, which is to say, for furthering the assault on your body.[6]

Coates's emphasis on the black body and its vulnerability to structural vestiges of white supremacy is a form of mistaking the symptom for the disease and, as always with Coates, hyperbolically exaggerated. There is no denying, as Orlando Patterson argues in *Slavery and Social Death*, that the bodily characteristics of slaves and their freed descendants, from ancient Athens to Jim Crow–era America, were used as one of the justifications for their marginalization. Often the physical characteristics were associated with a threatening prowess—sexual, physical, or otherwise. Today, however, even beyond the success of the civil rights movement in demanding that blacks be treated equal before the law, the status of blacks and their cultural products have risen so much that some of the most dysfunctional aspects of black culture have been embraced by various segments of the white community. Take explicit rap music, for example. It's a billion-dollar industry that has gained mass appeal beyond its provincial origins in black New York of the Sugarhill Gang days in the 1980s. The genre celebrates all the behavioral dysfunction that continues to enfeeble the black community, and it has made the N-word fashionable here at home and abroad to boot.

For the sake of political motives, Coates exerts much effort to portray blacks as passive, innocent, and helpless, while he portrays whites as naïve but diabolical perpetrators. He glibly sets up a racial straw man for the sake of excusing the very real fear and physical threat he experienced trying to survive in his black Baltimore neighborhood. The demands of survival, according to Coates, took the form of learning another language "consisting of a basic complement of head nods and handshakes." Something as mundane as smiling, and whom one smiled at, carried symbolic significance in Coates's Baltimore neighborhood. A soft and unselfconscious demeanor was a sign of weakness in a black man, and an invitation to physical altercations. Coates had to memorize certain blocks to be avoided, and developed a "smell and feel of fighting weather." He refers to learning these survival skills as learning specific laws: "I recall learning these laws clearer than I recall learning my colors and shapes, because these laws were essential to the security of my body." Unfortunately, the time spent learning the laws of survival was time not spent on, as Coates says, the "beautiful things."[7] In other words, his street knowledge came at the expense of book knowledge.

Coates's honesty about the mental cost of trying to survive black ghetto culture is admirable, especially for someone who is as sensitive and intellectually inclined as he is. But in this part of the letter, his son would have benefited from an extended discussion of the emotional damage young black men do to themselves by adopting ghetto rules of behavior. Richard Major, professor of psychology at University of Wisconsin at Eau Claire, calls ghetto rules of behavior a "cool pose."[8] The cool pose is a type of speech and behavior that exaggerates masculinity. The studied indifference and aloof swagger of the pose stunts the emotional vocabulary of black males and makes it almost impossible for them to show vulnerability or the willingness to compromise in challenging situations. If Coates were not a racial ideologue, he would have admitted to his son that many fatal police encounters between young black men and the police are precipitated by a lethal standoff between a cool pose and law and order. Coates goes to great lengths in his letter to portray young black men as innocent victims of America's ritualistic slaughter of black bodies, while neglecting to mention the violent swagger displayed by young black men. In my opinion, the unfortunate deaths of many of these young men highlight both police misconduct and the black family's losing struggle to civilize its young boys.

The streets of Baltimore were not the only problem that conspired to limit Coates's development; his primary and secondary schooling also did so:

> The streets were not my only problem. If the streets shackled my right leg, the schools shackled my left leg. Fail to

comprehend the streets and you give up your body now. But fail to comprehend the schools and you give up your body later. I suffered at the hand of both, but I resent the schools more.

Why he resents the schools more is unclear. It has to do with the false morality in the "rote discipline" of the black body. The routines of his school days, such as walking in single file, standardized testing, memorizing theorems, copying directions, were one big subterfuge. The real intent of schools, according to Coates, is to lull Americans into forgetting that the American Dream rests on black bodies that are bloodied and broken.[9]

Having recognized that the streets and schools are "arms of the same beast," he begins to indulge his autodidactic tendencies as a way of interrogating the stories he heard in school. Coates's consciousness is awakened by the writings and speeches of Malcolm X and the hip-hop artists who often quoted the provocative lyrics of the slain black militant. The racial and intellectual inspiration that Malcolm X offered to him in the early '90s is palpable in his letter to his son. Malcolm X's sayings and phrases, such as, "Don't give up your life, preserve your life," "If you're black, you were born in jail," and "black is beautiful," were music to Coates's ears. Inspired by the personality and courage of Malcolm X and other black militants, he embarked on a journey of racial reclamation through books and his own study and exploration. He sums up his racial sentiments:

That was what I heard in the call to "keep it real." Perhaps we [blacks] should return to ourselves, to our own primordial streets, to our own ruggedness, to our own rude hair. Perhaps we should return to Mecca.[10]

Coates refers to Howard University as Mecca; several members of his family attended the school. He was admitted to the historically black college, although he eventually dropped out without getting a degree, and it was there that he was introduced to a wide range of black people and black experiences. But whereas the perspective of the more nuanced writer would have been enlarged by Howard University's cosmopolitan student body and faculty, Coates's preoccupation with the black body and its discontents is made all the more provincial by his interest in mediocre, racist, and fringy black writers. From the non-fringy black writers he was introduced to at Howard, Zora Neale Hurston, Frederick Douglass, and Stanley Crouch, he seems to have learned very little. Basically, the Coates that we get during his Howard University days is the Coates channeled through less capable, but just as hateful, writers of today. *Between the World and Me* is a feeble attempt to speak truth to power, but instead it speaks defeatism and a warped view of America to a son. One can only hope that Ta-Nehisi Coates's son will outgrow his father's shackles.

We are now in a better position to reflect on why Brooks and his crowd felt the need to genuflect before Coates's racial chauvinism. Coates speaks to a deep vulnerability in the national psyche of Americans, especially elite white Americans. For a fair-minded person, it's easy to look at American history, see the indignities and brutality African Americans have endured, and feel morally sick. It's just as easy to see that African Americans have done a hell of job with the circumstances they initially found themselves in, but that they are no different from other ethnic groups in America who strive to rise above their humble beginnings. Yes, the majority of African Americans were introduced to America through slavery, but they were not permanently scarred by the experience of slavery.[11] They are not in need of constant moral cheerleading from their betters. Unfortunately, they are portrayed otherwise in today's America. In fact, the most pernicious ideas in the public square today are usually expressed on behalf of minority communities, and African Americans in particular. There is no tiptoeing around this fact. Racial and ethnic minorities, but African Americans especially, have been portrayed by a broad swath of elites, especially white elites, as the vanguard of righteous forces that seek to dismantle a systemic racist America and what it stands for. When left-leaning elites speak about diversity, equity, and inclusion (DEI), defunding the police, the benefits of non-traditional family formations, the elimination of single-family zoning, each of these issues are spoken of positively with the same disclaimer: *These developments are good because people of color, and African Americans in particular, face systemic racism on a daily basis.*

Today's Left is viscerally opposed to those who think differently from them on the issue of race, as it seeks to dominate and control the narrative in the public square. I believe these sentiments arise from the fact that those on the Left like the David Brookses of the world often "feel" their politics; it serves a deep emotional need. There's something to be said for feeling one's politics, not just parroting political platitudes; purveyors of opinion on the Right also need to appeal to their audience on an emotional as well as an intellectual level. Given this fact, what are conservatives up against in American culture, and do we have the wherewithal to stop America's cultural drift further and further to the left? In Critical Race Theory, identity politics, the Black Lives Matter movement, and various efforts to defund the police, we see a concerted effort by those on the Left, like Coates, to obscure a healthy love of country that most Americans—except those who wallow in a racialist mindset—intuitively feel.

There is nothing more predatory than ideologies designed to deny a child his American birthright. But there is hope considering recent political developments. We seem to be witnessing a bottom-up movement to take back the country across this great land. From Florida to Texas to Colorado, pockets of resistance are emerging in the political arena on issues of merit, discrimination, free speech, and gender. These political winds are an organic response to a set of elite cultural beliefs and practices that seek to alienate children from their family, community, and country.

Most African Americans are hardworking, committed to fair play, and deeply rooted in the spirit of 1776 and 1863. As an African American, to see my community portrayed as perpetual foes of traditional American beliefs and practices by elites, white and black, is painful. What makes this racial dynamic so insidious is that it creates bewildered feelings in all Americans. To notice that a significant number of black and white elites are opposed to traditional American values is frowned upon in polite circles. Such feelings inevitably lead to resentment, guilt, and paralysis. Conservative African Americans who notice are quickly marginalized and treated as community outcasts. All the while, American history continues to be revised, statues get yanked down, and children continue to get segregated based on their perceived "privilege."

For the good of America and its future, this racial dynamic must stop. Conservatism is positioned to stop the madness, and to begin the work of promoting an American cultural renewal based on individual agency and color-blindness. The ideas of agency and color-blindness need to be embraced in America now more than ever. Over the past three decades, the conceptual frameworks in which race has been discussed—multiculturalism, Critical Race Theory, or wokeism, and antiracism—have steadily challenged just those ideas of individual agency and color-blindness. But renewal is only possible if conservatives insist that America has one civic culture, not many, and that there will be no privileging of one racial group over another.

CHAPTER 8

Ibram X. Kendi

"Antiracist baby learns all the colors, not because
race is true. If you claim to be color-blind, you deny
what's right in front of you."

Ibram X. Kendi

The anti-color-blind message that comes through loud and clear in the writings of Derrick Bell and Ta-Nehisi Coates is one of racial division, segregation, and deep anti-Americanism. Not to be outdone, Ibram X. Kendi, the most glib and vacuous of the three writers, has developed his own race cottage-industry in opposition to color-blind principles. The majority of Kendi's writings revolve around the ideas of "antiracism" and the "antiracist." He defines the antiracist in his book How to Be an Antiracist as "One who is supporting an antiracist policy through their actions or expressing an antiracist idea." He goes on to explain that an antiracist policy would be "policy designed to dismantle racial hierarchies, or one that promotes racial equity. All of this seems obvious and on the face of it unobjectionable. Where Kendi reverts to racial demagoguery is when he claims that it's pointless for a person to say they're "not racist." It's not enough to "not be a racist," according to Kendi—one must been antiracist. There to middle ground, argues

CHAPTER 8

Ibram X. Kendi

"Antiracist baby learns all the colors, not because race is true. If you claim to be color-blind, you deny what's right in front of you."[1]

Ibram X. Kendi

T he anti-color-blind message that comes through loud and clear in the writings of Derrick Bell and Ta-Nehisi Coates is one of racial division, segregation, and deep anti-Americanism. Not to be outdone, Ibram X. Kendi, the most glib and vacuous of the three writers, has developed his own race cottage industry in opposition to color-blind principles. The majority of Kendi's writings revolve around the ideas of "antiracism" and the "antiracist." He defines the antiracist in his book, *How to Be an Antiracist,* as "One who is supporting an antiracist policy through their actions or expressing an antiracist idea."[2] He goes on to explain that an antiracist policy would be a policy designed to dismantle racial hierarchies, or one that promotes racial equity. All of this seems obvious, and on the face of it, unobjectionable. Where Kendi reverts to racial demagoguery is when he claims that it's problematic for a person to say they are "not racist." It's not enough to "not be a racist," according to Kendi—one must be an antiracist. There's no middle ground. To be antiracist is morally praiseworthy; to not be a racist or to be a racist is morally equivalent and, thus, morally blameworthy. If one is not actively engaged in activities that are antiracist, one is a racist. Neutrality or color-blindness on the issue of race is equivalent to racism:

> [C]laiming "color blindness" is akin to the notion of being "not racist"—as with the "not racist," the color blind individual, by ostensibly failing to see race, fails to see racism and falls into racist passivity. The language of color blindness—like the language of "not racist"—is a mask to hide racism.[3]

His ideology and the political movement it represents are, on the most basic level, antithetical to individual autonomy and the individual rights enshrined in the Bill of Rights. Freedom of conscience or civil liberties can't be extended to blatant racists. In a manner similar to the doctrine of faith and works in a religious context, here unless individuals can show through their faith and works a commitment to the antiracist cause, they are irredeemably racist, and must be dealt with as racists. In the political context, too, the standard of adjudicating the soundness of law or policy isn't determined by constitutional principles, the judicial process, or even natural law: it's whether the law or policy is deemed antiracist. Law that discriminates on the basis of race is considered lawful as long as it discriminates for the sake of equity. The racial powers that be, according to Kendi, have wielded the term "racial discrimination" in an indiscriminate manner. All discrimination is not wrong. As Kendi says, "if discrimination is creating equity, then it is antiracist."[4] Within his racist/antiracist view, there's no limit to how far the racist label extends, as long as it furthers the goals of the antiracist. For all practical purposes, the term antiracist becomes a moral wrecking ball for everything thing that stands in opposition to its goals. After all, who wants to be called a racist?

The real-world implications of the antiracist thesis are the modern segregationist trends we see today in many parts of our society. Affinity groups have emerged in the last several years in primary school settings all the way up to institutions of higher education. One local school in Kentucky advertises the nature and purpose of its affinity groups as "a group of people who share a similar identity. . . . The group is a place for reflection, dialogue, and support; it ultimately strengthens ties within the community."[5] All very innocuous sounding. Hardly! These groups exist to foster divisiveness, mainly along the lines of race, gender, and sexuality. The race- or ethnic-based affinity groups for African Americans, Native Americans, Hispanic Americans are particularly problematic because of the historical backdrop of marginalization that competes, psychologically, with the factual progress each of these groups has realized over the past half century in terms of material well-being and perceived status. Racial and ethnic affinity groups, with the endorsement of institutional administration, foster a sense of separateness and, ultimately, grievance on the part of those inside the group toward those outside the group, and resentment toward those in the group from those outside of it who don't share the identity of the group in question. So Kendi gets it precisely backwards in his rejection of race-neutrality or color-blindness in the pursuit of racial equity. He argues that " ... all ethnic groups, once they fall under the gaze and power of race makers [white people], become racialized."[6] Policies that promote color-blindness can deracialize thinking among groups so that shared goals and values become the ground on which a nonracial consciousness emerges—to the benefit of all parties involved. In short, the goal is not to talk about race more, which is what antiracism's race-based affinity groups do. It's to talk about race less.

A related issue that stems directly from antiracism, and portends a lot of ethnic, racial, and constitutional conflict on campuses in the years ahead, is the push to require faculty, staff, and students to sign diversity statements. The requirement doesn't just apply to present faculty, staff, and students, it also applies to prospective adjunct hires, staff, tenure track positions, and students. On other campuses, a personal diversity statement is required as a part of an applicant's dossier for employment. The statement details how a candidate's experience and background have contributed to promoting diversity in various contexts. In either case, diversity statements effectively operate as ideological statements that are antithetical to both excellence in any traditional understanding of the word, but also antithetical to the true meaning of the nation's creed "that all men are created equal," and to the constitutional principles of religious liberty and equality before the law. Accordingly, antiracism's DEI ideology operates on two claims: America is systemically racist, and it is white Americans who perpetuate racial oppression against people of color, particularly against black Americans. These statements aren't just harmless, procedural niceties designed to give administrators "something to do." They come with incentive structures, budgets, and penalties. A quick online search of DEI at universities and colleges yields what appears to be the consensus view on diversity statement requirements and the future goals for its implementation.

- Establish expectations for faculty and staff for contributions to an inclusive college climate (Outcomes: Diversity activities tracking is now included in faculty annual evaluations)

- Diversity and inclusion criteria in annual evaluations for faculty and staff
- Number of students, staff, and faculty participating in diversity-related professional development

Given my tenure in academia over the last twenty years, I can attest to the view. On most college campuses across the country, there is some equivalent of the diversity statement requirement. Inevitably, diversity statements will wrongly challenge some students' and faculty members' consciences. They will also put faculty and students in a very uncomfortable and financially precarious position for themselves and their families. Some of the examples that I have in mind aren't difficult to imagine. Consider a prospective hire or new student expressing reservations about the claim that "the only remedy for past discrimination is present discrimination," as they may (rightly in my view) believe that if discrimination is a problem, we need to stop discriminating, not shift to a different (and "approved") target group. Similarly, a prospective hire or student may express concerns about assertions that all members of a particular race (whites) are racists, as they may (rightly in my view) resist the notion that all members of a group can be summarily characterized with a pejorative term solely on the basis of their skin color. They may, in fact, argue that this is the very thing we ought not to be doing if we take racial justice seriously either as individuals or as an institution. These quite reasonable views conflict with the prevailing anti-white dogma that is espoused in antiracism's DEI ideology. I am not arguing that discussions of race and racism be silenced (such discussions and their arguments should be allowed to stand or fall on their own merits). I simply believe that the views opposed to antiracism's assumptions must be part of the discourse—they cannot be tacitly or explicitly held as "forbidden." The stakes are too high, and the stakeholders to whom we are responsible (students) are far too diverse to defend a racially biased approach to complex historical and social issues.

One other real-world implication of taking Kendi's antiracism seriously is that it forces its advocates to simplify phenomena that are multifaceted and complex by nature. Kendi's every utterance involves one glib explanation after another of complex ideas and phenomena. His naïvete is on full display when he discusses cultural differences between racial and ethnic groups. In a number of different contexts, he argues that the cultural antiracist position holds that cultural standards must be rejected, while at the same time effort should be directed toward equalizing cultural differences among racial groups. What he has in mind is that African Americans should reject "white cultural standards" that necessarily put them at a disadvantage within a racial hierarchy that deems African American culture pathological. His larger point is that any differences in outcomes that exist between African Americans and other groups is due to systemic racism. In fact, he goes so far as to propose an antiracist constitutional amendment. The amendment "would make unconstitutional racial inequity over a certain threshold. . . ."[7] The assumption behind the hypothetical amendment is that racial inequity is *ipso facto* due to racist policy because racial groups, absent discrimination, are equal and should have equal outcomes in education, productivity, status, etc., across the board. Of course, this assumption is not only naïve, it's silly. For the sake of civility, I'll take the assumption seriously and explain why it's wrongheaded even as a hypothetical.

Although not as sophisticated, Kendi's line of argument against group differences in outcome is very similar to the type of arguments promoted by a number of other public intellectuals and academics. Examples include "luck egalitarians," John Rawls and his redistributionist kin, all of whom propose various conceptions of equal opportunity and various schemes to socially engineer desired outcomes.[8] Often these conceptions of equal opportunity blindly assume that most of the differences in achievement between individuals and racial groups should either be even or random. In the case of luck egalitarians, advocates of an extreme version of equal opportunity, life chances should depend only on an individual's responsible choices, not on brute luck. Brute luck would include things like one's genetic endowment, abilities, and the circumstances one is born into. Each of these factors would be considered morally illegitimate because they are unchosen; they are the result of brute luck. On the other hand, luck egalitarians deem things that are acquired by an individual, both tangible and nontangible, through deliberate and calculated choices, as morally legitimate. The equal opportunity view that Kendi, luck egalitarians, and others express goes wrong in automatically assuming that, if it weren't for discrimination, the achievements and outcomes of various racial groups would be random or even. Kendi insists upon this assumption.

He does so because the equal opportunity view takes it for granted, and rightly so, that the differences between racial and ethnic groups aren't due to genetic differences or a genetic determinism among groups. In the absence of a genetic explanation, it becomes all the more attractive to infer that disparities in outcomes that are not even or random can be explained by discrimination or some other form of malicious intent. Kendi doesn't consider that there are other factors, cultural factors, that lead to different outcomes among groups and group achievement. Contrary to Kendi and luck egalitarians, it is foolish to assume that equal opportunity requires that a group's path to achievement be completely devoid of obstacles that are not of their own choosing. Brute luck and its effects are not episodic; they are factors throughout one's life. The economist, Thomas Sowell, sums up the issue succinctly by emphasizing that it is cultural traits that account for differences among ethnic groups and that culture is intangible and portable. Culture includes not only customs, values, and attitudes, Sowell argues, but also skills and talents that more directly affect economic outcomes, and which economists call human capital:

> To account for radical differences in income and wealth among groups living in the same society, environment can be defined as what is going on around a group, while culture means what is going on within each group.[9]

More than skills are involved in differentiating various racial and ethnic groups. More important, behind the skills are cultural values that make the acquisition of new skills a priority, and values that make the shedding of obsolete skills imperative—which shows that cultural differences among groups are not random or even.

Antiracist ideology is tailor-made for the guilt-prone, white, upper middle class. The reason for this has something to do with the moral complacency that haunts this class of Americans, as chronicled in Charles Murray's book *Coming Apart*. The other factor that accounts for the racial guilt among this class seems to be a softness or shallowness that gets assuaged by allying itself to causes often contrary to its self-interests. The African American cause in particular promises so many complexities and complicated feelings, especially the feeling of guilt. I'm only speculating here, but I think there is some merit to what I'm saying. Beyond speculation, what I'm absolutely clear on is that Kendi has cleverly tapped into these emotions among white Americans. The ancient Greeks had a word for this type of wicked cleverness: *deinos*. It describes a set of personal characteristics, or a skill set, used competently and cleverly for sordid ends or goals. The presumed motive of Kendi's fits this description. Aside from particular white Americans, some African Americans, too, have embraced antiracism. The reason for this isn't much of a mystery. African Americans who peddle some version of antiracism are either racist against white people and/or simply comfortable using antiracist ideology as a political bludgeon to paralyze their opponents for monetary, social, cultural, or political gain. To put it bluntly, whites use it for the thrills of abnegation without any real sacrifice (without the hairshirt). Blacks use it mostly for financial gain.

It's no surprise that someone like Kendi would propagate an idea like antiracism. Similar to Coates and, to a lesser extent, Bell, Kendi was raised by parents who were race conscious in a political sense. This sense of consciousness shouldn't be mistaken as a benign appreciation of African Americans and their cultural accomplishments. The race consciousness that Kendi recounts being modeled by his parents is the Malcolm X, Stokely Carmichael, James Cone type of race consciousness.[10] It's the worst kind of race consciousness because it politicizes and pulverizes through its insistence on reducing all human relations to issues of race and racism. No doubt, this type of race consciousness accounts for Kendi questioning the motives of Justice Amy Coney Barrett for adopting two children of color. If you recall, in the context of Justice Barrett's nomination to the Supreme Court, Kendi went out of his way to emphasize that just because people like Justice Barrett have black children doesn't mean they can't be racist. In a tweet on September 26, 2020, he followed up by saying: "Some White colonizers 'adopted' Black children. They 'civilized' these 'savage' children in the 'superior' ways of White people, while using them as props in their lifelong pictures of denial, while cutting the biological parents of these children out of the picture of humanity."[11] Both the intended target of Kendi's words and the implication of his comments are clear.

✑

Antiracism ideology has completely taken the concept of character out of the discussion of race and racism. Think about this for a second. The civil rights movement at its core is about morally incentivizing a particular type of behavior based upon core American principles. It's about treating every American with respect and basic kindness. Believing that all Americans, white or black, are the same with respect to their moral capacities, unless and until their actions prove otherwise—and need to be treated the same—is essential. Character is everything. It's all you really have at the end of the day. How you treat others is reflective of your character. But antiracism and its racist offshoots, Critical Race Theory, and DEI are pushing for the opposite. Their advocates seek to barter our hard-won racial progress for sinecures and other personal aggrandizements. They want different things for different people, and the tradeoff will be different treatment. Antiracism and DEI, in particular, teach our educators to stop talking about character because the diversity trainers know that the topic of character interferes with their lazy effort of picking the low-lying fruit of race. It's no wonder that American children are not learning the Golden Rule in some schools. The Golden Rule was once taught in every elementary classroom. It states: "Do unto Others as You Would Have Them Do unto You." The assumption is that we are all equal and that our character will determine how we are treated or can expect to be treated. It states a basic universal standard that is essential in every religion: character matters.

Now that we have moved several years away from the death of George Floyd, an event that accounts for the feverish popularity of antiracism immediately following that tragic event, we now clearly see that Kendi's ideas are in direct opposition to Martin Luther King's ideas on race, racial freedom, the Constitution, and character. Everything that Kendi stands for contradicts constitutional principles, which is why he glibly questions and dismisses them repeatedly, while also dismissing the counsel of religion in public life. When it is all said done, Kendi's antiracism thesis is pro-racism and pro-permanent division of the races. It's an extension of Derrick Bell's and Ta-Nehisi Coates's cynical attitude towards racial fraternity.

For Kendi, we cannot all get along in America, and we never will. The only solution is to get rid of the country itself or radically revise it beyond recognition.

CHAPTER 6

Robin DiAngelo

> "To challenge the ideologies of racism such as individualism and color-blindness, we as white people must suspend our perception of ourselves as unique and/or outside race."
>
> *Robin DiAngelo*

The trend that emerges from the opponents of the color-blind approach to race relations is an abiding disdain for enlightenment concepts such as neutrality, objectivity, humanitarianism, equality, individualism, and formalism. Each of these concepts were mentioned by name as a source for the perpetuation of racism. Color-blind opponents argue that any talk of color-blind parlance couched in the language of neutrality or formalism obscures racial power structures designed to exploit non-white people. Despite the fact that the European Enlightenment as a political movement brought some dramatic concepts. The objectivity and impartiality, as in the context of law, were crucial to the modern-era efforts of extending the notion of equality to broader segments of the population in Western societies. Take, for example, the philosophic principles contained in the Declaration of Independence. As I have pointed out, the principles contained in the document were crucial

CHAPTER 9

Robin DiAngelo

"To challenge the ideologies of racism such as individualism and color blindness, we as white people must suspend our perception of ourselves as unique and/or outside race."[1]

Robin DiAngelo

The trend that emerges from the opponents of the color-blind approach to race relations is an abiding disdain for enlightenment concepts such as neutrality, objectivity, impartiality, equality, individualism, and formalism. Each of these concepts are mentioned by name as a source for the perpetuation of racism. The color-blind opponents argue that any talk of color-blind principles couched in the language of neutrality or formalism obscures racist power structures designed to exploit non-white people. Despite the fact that the European Enlightenment as a political movement had some drawbacks, concepts like objectivity and impartiality, mostly in the context of law, were crucial to the modern era's efforts at extending the notion of equality to broader segments of the population in Western societies. Take, for example, the philosophical principles contained in the Declaration of Independence. As I have pointed out, the principles contained in the document were decisive in the abolitionists' arguments against the institution of slavery. Those same principles provided the justification for the modern civil rights movement, among other movements in the Western hemisphere, many decades later. Both the principles and the movements those principles inspired emerged out of the philosophical firmament of the Enlightenment. Lord Chief Justice Mansfield's 1772 decree in the *Somerset* case originated out of those principles. Justice Harlan's 1896 dissent in *Plessy v. Ferguson* originated out of those principles.

The opponents of color-blindness are working tirelessly, by word and deed, to convince America to turn its back on those very same Enlightenment principles that have served freedom-loving African Americans and white Americans with the tools to overcome the tribalism and racial division in our not-so-distant past. One group of influential opponents of color-blindness is the diversity trainers. This group isn't influential because its arguments against color-blind principles are different or any more persuasive than Derrick Bell's, Ta-Nehisi Coates's, or Ibram X. Kendi's racist arguments have been; its arguments are influential because their reach is more widespread than the latter three writers' reach. After having been welcomed with open arms in the academy and then in corporate boardrooms following Title VII of the Civil Rights Act of 1964, diversity trainers are now found in the workplace of nearly every sector of American society. The original role of the diversity trainer was to augment civil rights legislation by making sure employers treated all their employees equally in terms of hiring, promotion, compensation, and training. The role evolved over the decades, culminating in the 1970s with the Social Security Administration mandating on a wide scale that their employees undergo racial bias training.[2] From then on, mostly by administrative fiat, diversity trainers have become full-fledged attachés of the anti-color-blind diversity industry.

Like most of the official pronouncements explaining the purpose of an institution's diversity practices, be it CRT, antiracism, or affinity groups, the descriptions are always innocuous sounding. Typical in this respect is the recently updated article on Penn State's Extension homepage, "What Is Diversity Training?" The authors describe diversity training as:

> ... intentional professional training designed to develop skills needed to facilitate working and interacting with people from diverse cultural backgrounds. A diversity training program aims to boost participants' awareness about different types of diversity, appreciating differences among co-workers, and provide knowledge and strategies ... to help build a positive work environment.[3]

In the description, notice which words are used and how there is no specificity about the nature of the diversity that's being promoted, and to whom it applies. Questionably, it assumes that diversity in the workplace is an unalloyed good. Aside from that not-so-obvious assumption, it fails to make clear that the historical impetus of facilitating "working and interacting with people" concerns white people's attitude and treatment of people of color, particularly black Americans. In a section of the article on the methodology of diversity training, the authors are more straightforward in their description of the aim of the people involved in boosting participants' awareness.

Diversity training seeks to develop empathy with minority/diverse groups to "improve pro-diversity attitudes and behavioral intentions toward these groups."[4] This latter claim is more consistent with the actual practice of diversity training sessions. The sessions are designed to develop an empathetic attitude toward minorities by casting white people as unintentionally harming people of color through their unconscious bias. Unconscious biases are ways that groups perceive one another, or stereotypes groups apply to one another, without a full awareness at the conscious level of these perceptions or stereotypes.

It's important to understand that the words "unconscious bias" have a stipulated definition in the practice of diversity training. A stipulated definition is one that specifies a specific meaning, or conditions, of a word's usage. In the context of diversity training, unconscious bias's stipulated definition is that certain motivational factors, choices, and actions that white people aren't fully aware of account for the structural barriers, both mentally and physically, that prevent people of color, especially blacks, from living a flourishing, productive life. In other words, social disparities that exist between whites and blacks are due to unconscious racism on the part of white people, and so training them to understand the lived experiences of minorities by developing "empathy with minority/diverse groups to improve pro-diversity attitudes and behavioral intentions" is the goal of diversity training. The possibility that minorities, too, could be biased in their motivations, actions, and choices toward white people or that social disparities experienced by them could be due to internal, cultural factors specific to the minority in question isn't entertained as a pro-diversity strategy. Ignoring these possibilities highlights just how biased diversity training is. Additionally, in ignoring these possibilities, diversity training operates under a framework that is antithetical to certain Enlightenment concepts that have been defining

features of the American project, and that also serve as the foundation for the color-blind approach to race relations I'm advocating.
Namely, it prioritizes group rights over individual rights; it prioritizes
ascriptive qualities like race over status derived from one's own efforts
(merit); it prioritizes "positive racial discrimination" to right historical wrongs over ending discrimination "now" through emphasizing
equality, neutrality, objectivity, and impartiality in the formulation
and application of law and public policy.

All of these antithetical features are on stark display in Robin
DiAngelo's book, *White Fragility: The Challenges of Talking to White
People about Racism*. As a diversity trainer herself, DiAngelo's book
typifies the anti-color-blind assumptions and practices of the diversity industry as a whole today. The ugliest aspects of tribalism and
racial atavism, features that characterize the industry, are presented
by DiAngelo as good and necessary in the quest to heighten the racial
consciousness of her intended audience: the white middle upper
class. As she puts it, it's precisely because she's a white American who
had previously been ignorant of race, but is now very conscious of
it, that she's able to reveal to her white audience the myopic perspective they have on race and its effect on themselves and, more important, people of color. As she puts it:

> I am a white American raised in the United States. I have
> a white frame of reference and a white worldview, and I
> move through the world with a white experience. My expe-
> rience is not a universal human experience. It is a particu-
> larly white experience in a society in which race matters
> profoundly. . . . But exploring these cultural frameworks

can be particularly challenging in Western culture precisely because of two key ideologies: individualism and
objectivity.[5]

Her problem with individualism, especially acute in white
Americans, is the age-old structuralist argument that says the naïve
among us believe that their actions are due to their own efforts, and
that the ascriptive qualities that define them socially—race, class,
gender—have very little sway over how they exercise their capacities
to express themselves, to express their characters, as they see fit as
individuals. DiAngelo's position is that individuals belong to groups
first and foremost. These groups define how we see ourselves, as
individuals, in relation to other groups. Groups make relative comparisons as opposed to absolute comparisons. Absolute comparisons focus on the unique cultural aspects of a racial or ethnic group
and how others might learn from and appreciate how those aspects
contribute to the common weal. Instead, much of the racial tension
that diversity training provokes is due to the nature of relative comparisons that are made during the sessions, which are conducted in
a way that sees the relations between white Americans and people of
color, particularly black Americans, as a zero-sum contest for economic and political power. And considering the historical record is
read as favoring white people, diversity training gets super-charged
in recognition of that history. In America, people of color are the
victims of white victimizers.

Relative comparisons, as opposed to absolute comparisons,
become the primary way groups acquire self-esteem and group pres-
tige. One's group provides a script, if you will, through which his
individuality gets expressed. The script that remains a constant for
white Americans, according to DiAngelo, the one that gets communicated through magazines, books, songs, television, and movies, is

one that communicates to every white person in relation to people of color, we are "better" than them.[6] These blanket assumptions about the way white people think are emblematic of DiAngelo's racial reductionism. (God forbid that DiAngelo's racial liberalism flips to racial resentment one day. She would be an articulate spokeswoman for common sense on racial matters.)

As a consequence of prioritizing the group over the individual, the diversity industry shuns objectivity and impartiality. The industry's reasoning, as characterized by DiAngelo, is that the web of racialized relationships among groups in American society makes it inevitable that our perspectives as individuals are limited by our group membership in a racial group.

> If group membership is relevant, then we don't see the world from the universal human perspective but from the perspective of a particular kind of human. In this way, both ideologies are disrupted. Thus, reflecting on our racial frames is particularly challenging for many white people, because we are taught that to have a racial viewpoint is to be biased.[7]

DiAngelo has conflated the meaning of the words universal and objectivity. Group membership in a racial group isn't relevant in all circumstances, but its irrelevance in those circumstances doesn't mean the perspective we bring to bear there is universal—it's not. It does mean, however, that the perspective we bring to bear is objective. It means that there must be, at a minimum, a set of epistemic standards that govern the relationships between groups if communication is to be productive. Such standards are the ones I've associated with the enlightenment tradition of rational discourse like impartiality and objectivity. In other words, the perspectives we bring to bear in relation to other groups require that we put aside, or bracket, our differences in order to be impartial or neutral with regard to our own biases and predilections. The goal is to bridge the gap in perspectives between groups, which means to rise above a "particular" perspective. Relationships are fraught with confusion, tension, and posturing when they are governed by irrational standards that essentialize individuals based upon their racial characteristics. What I mean by essentializing is the view that takes an aspect of a person—one's race, for example—as vital to who he is as an individual, whereas the other properties or characteristics of the person are much less vital or simply accidental features. The diversity training industry operates under the essentializing assumption that we are, as individuals, reducible to our racial group and the racial perspectives that define the group.

Additionally, DiAngelo uses the word "frames" to characterize the racialized perspective through which white people in America see themselves in relation to the others. It's important here to understand frames, because diversity training emphasizes racial frames as if they supervene upon all social discourse among people of a different race or ethnicity. They do not. The construction of frames typically emerges from framing questions or issues in a specific way to enhance the chances of achieving a desired end. In the diversity training context, similar to the decision-making context, frames must be broad enough to clarify the situation, encompass the situation's goals, and highlight resources within the situation to limit the complexity of the subject matter under discussion. Both the application of framing effects and anti-color-blind pedagogy are seen in the following real-world account of a diversity training session.

A typical session begins with a somber narrative that explains that people of color, especially blacks, have grown up with unfortunate racial experiences that leave conscious and unconscious trauma. The attend-ees are told that the effects of these racially traumatic experiences can be anything from simple psychological stress to the impetus for making life-altering decisions. Persons of color may choose to pursue a less demanding career or forego certain educational opportunities because the racial trauma they experienced severely affected their confidence. The diversity trainer's main goal is to quiet white people by conducting the session under the assumptions that all black people experience racism, whether they know or not, and that white people just can't relate to such experiences. (These latter two points usually work to also quiet the black person who disagrees with the trainer's assumptions.) All the above conveniently sets the stage so that the white people in the room remain quiet and are therefore kept out of the conversation, lest they show their white privilege or the urge to speak for people of color or both. At this point in the session, the case for systemic racism begins in earnest, skeptical blacks are shamed into not speaking out in dis-agreement with the trainer or the racial victimhood narrative that's told, and, most important, white attendees now feel duty bound to remain quiet or they will be ostracized and called out.

It should be clear from this brief but real-world example of a diversity training session that there's no tolerance for alternative points of view, nor tolerance for any point of view other than the official racial line. There is no tolerance for white people to share how they could relate to people of color as human beings with human and tragic stories that we all share despite our racial or ethnic background. It doesn't matter that your grandparents barely survived the Holocaust after having lost the majority of your family members, or if you are disabled or severely overweight—white people will never know how it feels to be black, and white people will always be part of the problem, intentionally or unintention-ally. You cannot share your story about being married to a black person because you probably have been insensitive and careless and racist to your partner at some point. You cannot share stories about your biracial children because of the same situation and, besides, they are also part of the problem: they are part white. They cannot fully relate to black suffering either. And you can still be racist towards your own biracial children as a white mom, because you are told that you perpetuate racism whether you intend to or not. You benefit from your whiteness.

Although diversity training could be an effective tool to help attendees become more receptive to another person's struggles, whatever they are, diversity training in its present form certainly isn't a lesson in opening one's mind to another group's culture, religion, race, or lived experiences. The current diversity training focuses on convincing all attendees that whites manipulate and hoard the benefits of the economy, monopolize the national political agenda, the schools, and its curriculum. All of which becomes the basis for making the case for affinity groups, safe spaces, and race-based curriculums that divide courses and physical classes by race. If this sounds like separate but equal, it is. Allowing racial or ethnic "safe spaces," or spaces technically separate from white people (even though this is illegal—so schools have to say all people are welcome in the spaces, but only if they are "respectful" of people of color), is a form of segregation. The active encouragement of separating the races is deliberate and not a byproduct. It is purposefully taught in diversity training sessions, so that the attendees, after much internal struggle with their color-blind selves, especially if they're of a certain generation, eventually acquiesce to the encouragement of racial separation. The transformation of the attendees upon entering a diversity training session, from initially striving to be color-blind to becoming race conscious, and not in a good way, is really unfortunate. At first, most attendees naturally reject racial separatism and all notions associated with it, but then after they receive many hours of forced diversity training, they feel less comfortable disagreeing, because remember, the attendees have already been taught not to disagree or reject the ideas presented. Keep in mind that throughout the diversity sessions, the anti-color-blind pedagogy on race is reinforced, making white people in particular feel racially separate and confused about everything they purported to know about race previously. This confusion is especially felt by those who are Gen-Xers or younger. Chances are, they were raised having been taught not to judge people by the color of their skin.

Diversity training has become the Trojan horse of many racial ideas today that threaten to re-legitimatize the immoral and now unlawful practice of segregating the races, separate but equal, that was upheld in the 1896 *Plessy v. Ferguson* Supreme Court decision. In the days of old, the Jim Crow days, separate but equal was based on crude and racist beliefs about African Americans specifically, but people of color in general. The practice was state sponsored, and it was thought to be in the interest of the common good to keep the races apart due to their incorrigible differences. Any breach of or challenge to separate but equal was met with grave, often fatal, consequences. Although the threat of violence minimized daily resistance to separate but equal in the use of public facilities between black Americans and white Americans, it was public ostracism, custom, and tradition that worked most effectively at maintaining the status quo of silence instead of speaking out against the practice.

Spearheaded by today's diversity trainers like DiAngelo, we are encouraged by influential sectors of our society to separate racial and ethnic groups, all in the name of Critical Race Theory, antiracism, and diversity, equity, and inclusion. The separation we witness today is just as crude as the separation we witnessed in the past. Racial- and ethnic-themed affinity groups and safe spaces are no less offensive than signs that read "colored drinking fountains," "white drinking fountains." From administrators to corporate CEOs to academics, the intention of today's advocates of separate but equal is said to be pro-diversity, the acknowledgement of past wrongs. The brand of encouragement we hear from these supposed thought leaders exemplifies the same type of ostracism and silencing of critics in this twenty-first-century iteration of separate but equal, Jim Crow style practice, which make otherwise good people fearful of speaking up or acting according to their color-blind belief that separate is not equal.

The other similarity that exists between the days of separate but equal and today's opponents of color-blind principles is a rejection of concepts associated with the Enlightenment. Concepts that have been and continue to be a positive good in American life like individualism, equality, and objectivity. Each of these concepts are the very basis of the color-blind approach to race relations. These concepts do not require a super-human effort to embody. They require the desire to approximate a civilized standard, which is to say, they simply require a good-faith effort to embody. In a similar fashion, color-blindness requires a good-faith effort in our relations with racial and ethnic groups other than our own. The current racial regime, diversity trainers and all, requires the opposite. Groups are ascribed moral status based on their race or ethnicity. Typically, the apportioning of moral status plays out along the lines:

- White people are bad
- People of color are good
- African Americans are both good and beyond criticism

The current racial regime also takes it for granted that racism is ubiquitous, it's systemic, rendering any attempt at objectivity or impartiality in assessing individual motives, group dynamics, merit, law, public policy—naïveté. To any sensible person, all of this should set off alarm bells. It's a contemporary version of the ugly racial doctrine of separate but equal.

PART III

Restoring the Virtue of Color-Blindness

CHAPTER 10

Oikophobia

I f it's true that ideologies have root causes in familial or ancestral resentments, then we have come close to understanding the motivation of those who actively campaign against the principles of color-blindness. The most well-known of the anti-color-blind advocates I have discussed—Bell, Coates, Kendi—are African Americans. DiAngelo is white. She is well-known, too, but she derives her anti-color-blind cues from longstanding critiques African Americans have offered against color-blindness as an approach to race relations. If she weren't endorsed by leftist African Americans like Michael Eric Dyson and others of the same ilk, DiAngelo and other white advocates of anti-color-blind principles wouldn't be taken seriously. Ideologies of race in CRT, antiracism, and DEI all revolve around seemingly intractable issues that plague the African American community. In discussions of race and racism, we often include the moniker "people of color," and I have done that as well, but really, it's all about the status of African Americans in America today. Which brings me to my opening sentence above. The motivation behind the thinking of Bell, Coates, and Kendi, and those African Americans who embrace it, is a type of alienation with roots in hatred of the familiar. The alienation I have in mind is akin to the intellectual mindset that was characterized by the English philosopher Roger Scruton as the rejection of what's near and home-like:

> . . . a hatred of home, which has been a frequent disease among intellectuals. . . . He [the intellectual] sees that which is his "own," his inheritance, as alien; he has fallen out of communication with it and feels tainted by its claim on him. . . . Therefore he portrays his home as something Other. . . .[1]

Scruton named the phenomenon he describes above, which is mostly seen in the West, as oikophobia. The term is a combination of two ancient Greek words, *phobia* (fear, aversion) and *oikos* (home, house). The Oik, shorthand for those who suffer from oikophobia, is unmoored from his native soil, home, community, and country. Think of it as an imperious attitude toward his compatriots, coupled with a radicalization of the spirit of democracy. He feels sympathy for the *foreign* enemy and disdains his fellow citizens and their traditions. His loyalties are often universalist, avowedly rejecting the cultural particularities that distinguish him from foreigners. In the American context, the Oik has a deep disdain for America, its way of life, and its institutions. A very shameful, but memorable, illustration of oikophobia is Ta-Nehisi Coates's recollection of his reaction to the September 11 attacks found in his book *Between the World and Me*. After the attacks, Coates is standing on a rooftop with family and friends looking at the physical destruction the attacks caused. He remarks:

> . . . looking out upon the ruins of America, my heart was cold. . . . In the days after, I watched the ridiculous

pageantry of flags, the machismo of firemen, the over-
wrought slogans. . . . I could see no difference between the
officer who killed Prince Jones and the police who died, or
the firefighters who died. They were not human to me.
Black, white, or whatever, they were the menaces of nature;
they were the fire, the comet, the storm, which could—with
no justification—shatter my body.[2]

Most Americans, black and white, were profoundly distressed
and galvanized by the attacks on 9/11. We understood in that moment,
if not before, what American exceptionalism meant. The attacks
tugged at my heart in a way that is still difficult to articulate. Either
one felt a surge of patriotism by the attacks, or one didn't. Coates
obviously didn't, instead suffering a severe attack of oikophobia—the
fear of that which nurtures and protects us.

Scruton has done us a service by coining such a term, although
the phenomenon he describes seems to be as old as Western civilization itself. It results from cultural decadence brought on by excessive
personal and political freedom. Many civilizations have gone through
periods of personal and political excess.[3] Plato illustrates the concept
of oikophobia in several of his political dialogues, particularly in
relation to the sophists. But here it will suffice to mention a quip in
Book VIII of the *Republic* that captures the deep sentiments of oikophobia. In the passage, Socrates is commenting on how excessive
freedom in a democracy distorts the proper attitude its citizens
should have toward personal relations in their country and political
relations with non-citizens. He observes that a "resident alien or a
foreign visitor is made equal to a citizen, and he is their equal."[4] The
quip sums up nicely the *xenophilia* (the love of strangers) and *allo-
philia* (the love of the Other) embraced by the Oiks. They think it is
petty, unbecoming, to make distinctions between citizens and

non-citizens. According to the Oiks, the native inhabitants of a country shouldn't be entitled to prerogatives that the non-natives aren't entitled to.

In a similar way, the alienation from the broader American community among African Americans accounts for the embrace of color-conscious ideologies such as antiracism and the like. The ideologies are a lament, if you will; a byproduct of negative cultural factors that exist within the community itself. These factors retard the development of public affections among African Americans that are routinely seen and expressed in other communities in American life. Having affection for the whole—community and country—first begins with having had one's affections nurtured and developed by the part—family and neighborhood. If these beginnings are in any way attenuated or unable to transmit the proper values unimpeded to an individual or group, their affection for the whole will be warped. The political stateman Edmund Burke puts it best in his *Reflections on the Revolution in France*:

> To be attached to the subdivision, to love the little platoon
> we belong to in society, is the first principle (the germ as
> it were) of public affections.[5]

The anti-color-blind theories I've discussed, and the racial vulnerability that makes the African American community susceptible to these racist ideologies, has everything to do with the breakdown of the African American family. In previous chapters I've mentioned the ancient Greek idea that *the beginning of anything that grows or develops is already half the whole of that thing*. Burke's quote is all about beginnings. It's within the little platoon of the family that we learn to love ourselves, our neighborhood, our community, our city, our state and, most important, our country. So many of the social and personal ills that plague African Americans originate in the home, in the family. How can African Americans express patriotism properly when many haven't been taught in the home to have a proper understanding of it?

The topic of the African American family and its struggles has an extensive body of literature, both popular and academic. My concern here is not to delve into the research so much, but to offer a point of view, reflections, that seldom get discussed in both literatures, but are witnessed by any honest, sympathetic observer of African Americans.

The African Americans who most display the qualities of oiko-phobia, particularly its alienation from the familiar, are not centered within family networks of strong marriages that promote individual flourishing. Families with mothers, fathers, and whole siblings cradle and center individuals. These families model behaviors and direct natural desires toward their natural ends. When a family fails to per-form its function, its members seek other means to fill the void. The way that some young African Americans have handled the disorien-tation of having fractured families is to latch onto a variety of destruc-tive behaviors or racially exclusionary ideas that are color-conscious, not color-blind. They seek a false sense of belonging, for example, in gang-like settings or in racialized affinity groups. There are many exceptions to this characterization of the African American com-munity, but I'm speaking in general.

African Americans deserve to have centered lives built around healthy family relationships and to feel grounded in the communities in which they reside as accepted members of their towns, cities, states. Given this, it has always surprised me that African Americans aren't more confident, perhaps even a little arrogant, about their longevity in America. Outside of old-line WASP families, African Americans are some of the oldest Americans. They've had a cultural presence in America since its colonial period, albeit a compromised one. If any group in America today has autochthonous origins, it's African Americans. They truly are a biological and cultural product of the New World, that is, America.

African Americans have a right to feel proud and patriotic, and any ideology that contradicts this right is destructive and runs contrary to the drive for upward mobility that has motivated the group historically; this is all the more so for the smart ones or the talented tenth, as W. E. B. Du Bois would put it.[6] Derrick Bell was profoundly mistaken in his *Faces at the Bottom of the Well*. Being unhappy, feeling unfulfilled, under-educated, and feeling underserving is not inevitable for African Americans.

Regarding the institution of family, it is well documented that children are the healthiest when raised by their heterosexual, biological parents who love and care about them. Community activists and academics who contort themselves to justify ever-new iterations of family formation are only hurting the communities they think they're helping. Additionally, there is mounting evidence that children must have healthy relationships with both a mother and father if their developmental trajectory is to be a flourishing one in adulthood.[7] Having a healthy family experience leads to having a respectful attitude towards your community and fellow Americans, regardless of race. At one time, generations of past African Americans did experience casual racism and the constant stress of a life surrounded by people who disliked them because of the color of their skin. This knowledge should not be forgotten. But here, too, the intact African

American family served as a bulwark for its family members. It was a boot-strapping enterprise, and a very good one! It's difficult for oikophobia to take root in individuals from happy, stable, well-adjusted families. The intact African American family that fought for integration, color-blindness, family values, and overall well-being for the country pointed the way forward for the country as a whole, and it continues to pay dividends to society today. Furthermore, racial harmony in the public square will lead to a more positive experience for everyone, and if we must speak about "social justice," it should reflect the goal of interpersonal development coupled with better education through choice, healthy family experiences with one's family, and a society that strives to practice fairness, equality, and color-blindness.

African American alienation from the broader American community and the anti-color-blind ideologies that stem from it will persist until African American families are made whole, mostly by their own efforts, and are able to give their children all the psychological tools needed to be happy and successful adults.

CHAPTER 11

Race Conscious Policies:
Entitlement, Resentment, Alienation

I pointed out in chapter 3 that the underrepresentation of students of color, mainly African Americans, at universities and colleges accounts for most of the race conscious programs like the ten-percent plans. Other lesser-known race conscious programs like Prep for Prep or A Better Chance are pipeline programs designed to funnel high school students of color into elite colleges and universities. The programs are caustic instruments of social policy that end up alienating students of color. These programs have been failures, and most likely, unconstitutional. However, it's instructive to see the mindset that has resulted from the programs.

An older book, Anthony Abraham Jack's *The Privileged Poor: How Elite Colleges Are Failing Disadvantaged Students*, is a case study of sorts that's relevant to many of the issues I've touched on already.[1] In it, Jack inadvertently illustrates just how alienating and antagonistic race conscious policies have been on students of color entering college—"inadvertently" in that Jack's intention is not to argue for color-blind admission policies in higher education; far from it. In fact, Jack advocates affirmative action on college campuses to be geared toward students of color. For those opposed to race

conscious admission policies, Jack offers a vivid cautionary portrait
of the negative consequences of five decades of affirmative action
on minority students. For students of color, these policies have created an entitlement mentality, alienation, and resentment. A mentality we are just now in the position to meticulously uproot through
color-blind public policy.

Jack's argument is that it is well and good that elite campuses
continue to diversify their student bodies, but it is not enough. They
must also recognize that lower income students are diverse. Among
these students there are real cultural differences and levels of college
preparedness due to the quality of high schools from which they
graduated. These differences are captured in what he refers to as
the Privileged Poor and the Doubly Disadvantaged. The Privileged
Poor are lower-income graduates of wealthy private high schools
like St. Paul's School in New Hampshire and Phillips Academy
Andover in Massachusetts. These students, according to Jack, have
benefited from all the resources and opportunities their exclusive
high schools provided, from study abroad programs to language
immersion programs to contact with faculty with higher degrees. As
Jack puts it, "Lower income graduates from these schools enter college already accustomed to navigating elite academic arenas, already
familiar with the ways and customs of the rich. True, they are poor,
but they have the privilege of an early introduction to the world they
will enter in college." The Doubly Disadvantaged, on the other hand,
tend to be students of color and from local public high schools that
are under-sourced, racially and socioeconomically segregated, over-
crowded and chaotic. Often the teachers in these schools are younger,
inexperienced, and unsupported. According to Jack, when these students "first set foot on an elite college campus, it looks, feels, and
functions like nothing they have experienced before."[2] Jack would
know; he has firsthand experience with both groups. In 2007, he

graduated from Amherst College by way of Gulliver Preparatory school in Florida. Having transferred to Gulliver his senior year from a rough, local public high school, he says he learned to negotiate the world of wealth, class, and advanced degrees at the elite private school. Gulliver was his training ground for Amherst College.

The psychological assets possessed by the Privileged Poor, in contrast to the Doubly Disadvantaged, determine the academic and social trajectory of each group on elite college campuses. Jacks purports to illustrate, through campus interviews, how each group of students experiences a prestigious undergraduate institution. He does not identify the institution where he conducted his research; he simply refers to it as Renowned. From all indications, he is most likely referencing his alma mater, Amherst College. The interviews show that the Privileged Poor's cultural competence puts them at ease among the high academic demands of the college and the experiences and affluence of the student body. One interviewee, a Privileged Poor African American, typifies the role of cultural competence. She explains how she navigates discussions of travel among rich, white students:

> People travel a lot. In conversations with a lot of women, especially wealthier women, there's a lot of talk about Europe, South America, or "Oh, I was in France two weeks ago. Me and my family backpacked around wherever." When I was in high school, I got to experience these things with my friends. People were talking about their yacht, where they bought houses. . . . I learned how to engage in conversation, and the conversations are going similar ways in college. Especially after going to France, too.[3]

Doubly Disadvantaged students, on the other hand, often feel alienated on campus because they lack cultural competence. Typical of this type of student is Valeria, a working-class Latina who discusses with Jack her ambivalence about reaching out to her professors at Renowned:

> My being uncomfortable going to office hours: that's the social class thing. I don't like talking to professors one on one. That's negative because Renowned really wants you to be proactive. And raise your hand. And talk. Freshman year, I didn't say a word. . . . My dad would always teach me, "You don't want to get where you are based on kissing ass, right?"[4]

It is clear from Valeria's comments that her personal expectations and the expectations of Renowned are at odds. Both her family and the local public high school she attended reinforced a set of values and expectations that made it difficult for her to engage with her professors. Several other interviews with Doubly Disadvantaged students reveal, for example, that as college freshman they initially thought professors should not be disturbed during the hours posted on their syllabus as "office hours." Whereas the Privileged Poor freshmen, having graduated from academically and socially elite high schools, knew office hours meant just the opposite.

In addition to highlighting the differences between lower-income students on an elite college campus, Jack concludes by highlighting some of the common experiences that unite the Privileged Poor and the Doubly Disadvantaged at Renowned. Both groups are poor on a wealthy campus and, according to Jack, suffer from structural exclusion. One example of the exclusion he is referring to is the practice of suspending meal services on campus during spring break, a practice Jack has fought to change. The assumption at Renowned, according to Jack, is that all students either return home or travel during spring break. The Privileged Poor and the Doubly Disadvantaged have to remain on campus because they lack the funds to return home or have dysfunctional homes they cannot return to. Consequently, lower-income students are forced to spend what little money they do have on food for a week. Experiences like these unite the Privileged Poor and the Doubly Disadvantaged. However, the majority of Jack's book consists of pointing out the differences between these two groups of lower-income students at the elite college.

Overall, Jack's discussion of the two groups of students can be divided into two parts. The first part tells a compelling story about the role that "gateway institutions," like high schools, play in equipping students with the skills to flourish in college. In making his case, Jack is solidly in the sociological tradition of Shamus Rahman Khan and Binder and Wood. Each of these authors recognize that a student's cultural competence stems from broad institutional influences, not just from the family. The distinction between the Privileged Poor and the Doubly Disadvantaged, along with the illustrations of how both groups of students navigate elite college campuses, is insightful and contains potential avenues for further exploration. The second part devolves into a clumsy discussion of inequality, structural racism, and privilege. Nothing is wrong with these topics per se, but he seems intent on exaggerating and politicizing some of the issues he observed at Renowned. For example, he doesn't make it clear at all how the Doubly Disadvantaged end up at elite colleges in the first place. According to Jack, nearly half of the Doubly Disadvantaged report not participating in any college assistance programs in high school. I was left to wonder if these students bumbled their way into elite colleges. It takes effort and support to apply to a college or university, let alone an elite one. The more plausible possibility is that Doubly Disadvantaged students showed some promise at their local public high school, received support, and were encouraged to apply to an elite college. Unlike the Privileged Poor, who make it into elite schools through pipeline programs like Prep for Prep or A Better Chance, Jack portrays the Doubly Disadvantaged as if they have very little personal autonomy or drive in the face of pervasive "structural racism." Playing up the contrast, at times, between the privileged Poor and the Doubly Disadvantaged seems to account for some of the exaggeration in his analysis.

Jack's discussion of the closure of Renowned's cafeteria during spring break and its impact on the Privileged Poor and the Doubly Disadvantaged deserves comment. The point that needs acknowledging is that it is not always fiscally prudent to keep college dining halls consistently open during breaks and designated holidays because a very small percentage of students remain on campus during these periods. Even the most well-endowed colleges have budget constraints. Moreover, the funds needed to cover the cost of opening the dining hall during spring break might mean fewer lower-income students get accepted with full funding. Those who remain on campus—international students, athletes, lower-income students—typically make plans to feed themselves during the week the dining hall is closed. Jack's interviews with lower-income students who remain on campus during spring break suggest that the college's indifference toward their situation is motivated by privilege. Their argument is that Renowned is so used to catering to wealthy, white students, it fails to see that lower-income students of color are practically starving in their dorms. In fact, we are told that one of his interviewees fainted from a lack of food during spring break. We also are told that Renowned is a "food desert" during routine closures of the dining hall. It may not be privilege, but cost and student usage that could be the actual cause of the dining hall closing.

It is obvious to any but the perpetually aggrieved that Jack is arguing over relatively minor and local matters, and it is hardly an illustration of systemic racism in American higher education.

It is clear from Jack's remarks about the Privileged Poor and the Doubly Disadvantaged that he believes elite colleges have an obligation to obscure the real cultural differences between the wealthy and minority students on campus in order to make the latter feel comfortable. For Jack, it is not enough for elite colleges to have admitted the Privileged Poor and the Doubly Disadvantaged; to have initiated their inevitable upward mobility. He suggests that elite colleges must micromanage students' lives on campus, lest a chance encounter between students reveals a white privilege. However, the most important obligation of an elite college, any college for that matter, is to foster a civil learning environment, educate its students, and disabuse students of their entitlement mentality, especially minority students.

CHAPTER 12

Identity, Nationalism, and Race

I've spoken a lot about color-blind principles and the color-blind approach to race relations in America, but I have only mentioned in passing the connection between "identity" and color-blindness. Understanding the connection between these concepts is important because they entail one another. It's difficult to be color-blind if one's primary identity is defined by a self-regarding identity like race. To see oneself in this way is different from feeling pride about one's particular cultural inheritance. For example, it's a point of pride for me that most of the great jazz musicians have been African American. It would be racist of me to believe that *only* African Americans can be great jazz musicians (I'm a huge fan of David Brubeck). To hold such a belief is to say my primary identity *is* my racial identity. The proper way to think about identity, especially within the context of America's racially and ethnically heterogenous culture, is to see one's American identity as primary. What exactly does it mean "to see one's American identity as primary"? To answer this question it's instructive to remind ourselves what identity politics is, and what various communities have appealed to in the past to rally the broader American community to their side in order to secure political recognition or greater access to the political process.

The phrase "identity politics" gained momentum during the '60s and was often used as a term of derision referring to parochial interests motivated by the social background or orientation of a particular demographic group. Race, gender, religion, and sexual orientation became powerful vehicles through which the personal became the political. One only needs to think about the African American civil rights movement and the gay rights movement to understand what's distinctive about identity politics and what's not. Both movements sought equal protection before the law for their respective communities, and for their individual members to be treated with dignity and respect. As I've mentioned, Martin Luther King Jr.'s "Letter from a Birmingham Jail" is a powerful rebuke of segregation because it's designed to resonate with Americans by appealing to the same Founding American documents and Western philosophical texts that some southerners used to support segregation. It's difficult not to be moved by the letter. In speaking about the tension in the community created by his movement's direct-action program (sit-ins and marches) in Alabama, King puts himself on the side of Socrates as the constructive provocateur:

> I have earnestly opposed violent tension, but there is a type of constructive, nonviolent tension which is necessary for growth. Just as Socrates felt that it was necessary to create a tension in the mind so that individuals could rise from the bondage of myths and half-truths to the unfettered realm of creative analysis . . . so must we see the need for nonviolent gadflies . . . that will help men rise from . . . the dark depths of prejudice and racism. . . .[1]

His mentioning Socrates is par for the course. The letter goes on to mention moral concepts, classic books, and political figures that have been staples of Western and American political and moral discourse. Likewise, gay rights activists, too, appealed to Founding principles contained in the Declaration of Independence and the United States Constitution to argue for individual rights and greater representation in the political process. David Lampo makes this case in his book, *A Fundamental Freedom: Why Republicans, Conservatives, and Libertarians Should Support Gay Rights*, by advancing the thesis that "it's the defenders of gay rights . . . not their opponents, who are keeping faith with the . . . principles of free enterprise, limited government, and individual rights."[2]

While it's true that identity politics informed the demands of these two communities, it's important to appreciate, for my purposes, that both movements, at the time, appealed to a comprehensive and inclusive national identity (I say "at the time" because today a vocal minority within both of these communities have embraced and advocate for an especially pernicious type of identity politics based on race and sexual orientation). Such an identity helped each movement gain much needed support from a broad swath of America. This is what it means to see one's American identity as primary: across racial, ethnic, and religious differences, we have a common tradition of ideas, cultural practices, and beliefs that are *the* constitutive part of who we are as Americans. In other words, creedalism coupled with specific cultural practices defines America and what it means to be an American. The particularities, the preferences, the ascriptive qualities of one's identity are secondary, or should be secondary, if we are to take color-blindness and its concomitant American identity seriously. The creedalist's conception by itself grounds the American identity solely in propositional or notional ideas: constitutionalism, rule of law, and human equality. Creedalism without a cultural *putsch* is especially ineffective against racial identity politics.

Considering the importance of individual identity to American history, and the role it has played in defining our national character, it's surprising that identity is not a recurring topic of conversation among those right of center. Issues of identity are certainly recurring themes on the Left, often to the detriment of thinking (like the color-blind approach to race relations) that seeks to minimize differences among Americans. There are a few public intellectuals that have waded into the waters of identity and have thereby elevated the discussion in interesting and expansive ways.[3] Two in particular are Francis Fukuyama and the Israeli scholar Yael Tamir.

Fukuyama offers an historical account of identity in the West and how it's manifested in the twenty-first century. In his book *Identity: The Demand for Dignity and the Politics of Resentment*, he argues that liberal democracies are healthiest when they foster inclusive national communities, rather than a bunch of narrow identities among the aggrieved. And he offers several proposals designed to mitigate the pernicious effects of identity politics while also promoting an inclusive national identity. Reforming immigration and encouraging citizens to commit to national service—either in the form of serving in the military or in a civilian capacity—are two such proposals mentioned. The historical account of identity Fukuyama offers is fascinating and worth recounting. Tamir argues that nationalism, as a political movement, can be a unifying force to overcome ethnic, religious, and class divisions that plague the modern nation-state. Ironically, in exhorting liberals to reconsider the virtues of nationalism as a noble and enduring political orientation, Tamir makes a compelling case for serious conservatives. Despite the fact that her book *Why Nationalism* exhorts liberals to embrace nationalism, her insights are worth considering in connection with the color-blind approach to race relations.

Fukuyama and Western Sources of Identity

To begin, Fukuyama's approach to identity presupposes that human behavior on an individual level is motivated by factors other than just the ones commonly espoused by neoclassical economists. These economists argue that human beings are "rational maximizers" always in pursuit of their own preferences and utilities. Our individual preferences tend not to be rationally ordered in terms of a highest good, but are ordered emotively and only rationally pursued. On this view, material incentives are the main sources of human motivation and account for the human need for recognition. Classical Marxists also share the neoclassical economists' view. The difference is that Marxists believe classes rather than individuals pursue their economic self-interest. In this dispute, it seems the neoclassical economists were right. In communist China, for example, productivity on collective farms was low because peasants could not keep the surplus of what they produced. When the incentive structure was changed in the 1970s to allow peasants to keep their surplus, output soon doubled. We also see, according to Fukuyama, the role material incentives played in the 2008 financial crisis. Investment bankers were rewarded for risk taking and short-term profits—and that is what they pursued at the expense of stability. Fukuyama does not reject economic reasoning entirely. But he argues that the shortsightedness of the materialist view of human motivation is that it "does not satisfactorily explain either the soldier falling on the grenade, or the suicide bomber, or a host of other cases where something other than material self-interest appears to be in play. It is hard to say that we 'desire' things that are painful, dangerous, or costly in the same way we desire food or money in the bank." In other words, the materialist has a hard time accounting for supererogatory acts: acts that are heroic, that go above and beyond the call of duty, often requiring self-sacrifice.

In contrast to the materialist model of human motivation, Fukuyama offers a much older account that goes beyond bodily wants and material preferences. Fukuyama appeals to Plato's discussion of the soul in the *Republic* and the ancient Greek concept *thymos*, which is usually translated as *spirit*. In Book IV of the *Republic*, Plato divides the soul into three parts: the rational, the spirited, and the appetitive. Each part of the soul offers a specific type of human motivation. Reason motivates humans to figure things out; appetites motivate humans to satisfy basic desires (food, thirst, sex, and similar needs); spirit motivates humans to feel a sense of justice and demand rights and recognition. It strives for good repute and victory. Spirit can be characterized in the following way: it makes one competitive with others, usually for the sake of distinguishing oneself from the *hoi polloi*, to achieve worthy goals for oneself and one's society, typically within the context provided by society's scheme of values. Ultimately, spirit encourages pride in oneself and one's accomplishments, esteem for noteworthy others, and the desire to be esteemed by others and by oneself. Other academic philosophers, like Alasdair MacIntyre and Charles Taylor, have treated the issue of identity from a historical perspective; Fukuyama's approach is unique for a social scientist who typically prefers descriptive accounts over prescriptive ones. He juxtaposes the neoclassical or materialist account of human motivation with the ancient Greek conception and rightly concludes that the ancients recognized that "human beings do not just want things that are external to themselves, such as food, drink, Lamborghinis, or that next hit. They also crave positive judgment about their worth or dignity."[4] Judgment can come from within or from society's recognition of a person's worth. Fukuyama concludes that *thymos* or spirit is "the seat of today's identity politics."[5]

Yet not all individuals or groups desire to be seen as equals among others. Some have a desire to be recognized as superior (*megalothymia*), while others have a desire only to be recognized as having equal worth (*isothymia*). In other words, *thymos* is not expressed equally among all human beings, because individuals and groups often feel and act as if their identities are more equal than others' and should be recognized as such. Not until *thymos* was coupled with the idea that individuals have an inner and an outer self, and that the inner self "was more valuable than the outer self," did identity become crucially important.[6] According to Fukuyama, the disjunction between the true self or one's identity and the outside world occurred in the West during the Protestant Reformation and was expressed by Martin Luther. As a young man, Luther struggled with not knowing whether he was acceptable to God, and he later came to the realization that the Church and performing works "acted only on the outer person—through confession, penance, alms, and worship of saints—none of which could make a difference," because grace could only be bestowed by the love of God.[7] Luther came to the belief that man has two natures, a spiritual one and an outer bodily one, and that faith alone can save the inner man, not external works and their preoccupation with man's bodily nature. Despite Luther's belief in the dual nature of man, he was not calling for the true self or identity to be publicly recognized. The demand for public recognition of the inner self began with the philosopher Jean-Jacques Rousseau.

Rousseau secularized the inner self and set it at odds with society. The dynamic that emerged was a naturally good self with its identity intact in a struggle with the external social forces of a society that demands conformity to its dictates. In Rousseau's *Discourse on Inequality*, people feign qualities and contort themselves to appear to be something they are not and to gain advantage. There are rich and poor, servant and master. Such positions are only possible as people need each other. The property of the rich is insecure, which leads the rich to conceive of the plan of using the weak to defend them. The rich come up with the idea of civil society to protect property. The origin of society, according to Rousseau, is a ruse by the rich. The state is a tool for securing their interests. Rousseau then wondered if there can be any freedom in society. Perhaps if people were not softened too much by luxury and society, they could accept stern morality and live by reason. They would not be too dependent on each other and not live too much in the thoughts of others. If inequality could be based on real differences within the inner self, rather than conventional differences (the outer self), then perhaps freedom could exist in society. Fukuyama suggests that Rousseau's fascination with the depravity of existing society and the possibility of a radically different, free way of life ushered in a very modern question: "Who am I?" The question of identity thus combines three elements. The first element is *thymos*, the human need for recognition. The second element is the distinction between the inner and the outer self, and the inner self's antagonistic relationship to society. The third element is the democratization of identity, wherein recognition is due everyone. It was Georg Wilhelm Friedrich Hegel, according to Fukuyama, who first articulated in *The Phenomenology of Spirit* and *The Philosophy of Right*, the idea that the inner self is not simply one's personal reflection but rather that identity and its recognition should have standing under the law.

After having brought his argument up to this point, Fukuyama shows the real-world effects of questions of identity on political representation by showing the role identity plays domestically. Which is to say, the United States is not immune to issues of identity. Donald Trump's elevation to the presidency was made possible, in part, by the white working class. Stagnant wages, job loss, and social deterioration were some of the factors that motivated Trump voters. The most important factor, however, was what Fukuyama refers to as the "perception of invisibility."[8] The perception among these voters is that the loss of their middle-class status is due to an elite that is disdainful of them but supportive and sympathetic toward undeserving minorities and the poor. The perceived loss of status among the working class is not just about economic deprivation; it is mainly about the loss of a historical identity.

Fukuyama concludes his discussion of identity by asking, "What is to be done?" What can liberal democracies do to reverse the proliferation of self-regarding identity groups defined by race, gender, sexual orientation, religion, and politics? Fukuyama's proposals encourage the development of (1) broader identities that are integrative and promote mutual respect and dignity among citizens of liberal democracies; and (2) some form of national service that demands more from its citizens in return for protection of citizens' rights. Such service, says Fukuyama, would be premised on the fact that "citizenship requires commitment and sacrifice to maintain."[9] In effect, it would be a contemporary form of classical republicanism. Ultimately, Fukuyama's proposals amount to an endorsement of a "healthy nationalism." He does not describe his propositions as such, but a nationalism of this sort would be consistent with Fukuyama's other observations as well, especially his concern for the lack of assimilation among immigrants and the treatment of African Americans. I single out African Americans here because Fukuyama singles out the Black Lives Matter movement in passing as helping the United States become "more conscious" of the way it treats minority citizens.[10] His argument is only partly true. The Black Lives Matter movement has also shown that in the absence of a compelling and positive American national identity, antagonistic identities multiply and grievances mount.

As for Fukuyama's proposal to implement a national service requirement to foster a sense of national community, virtue, and public spiritedness, it is an interesting idea. It is true that with the rise of the all-volunteer military force there are very few places or institutions where young people socialize with those who are of a different social class or race, or from a different region of America. When young people do come into contact with one another, it is most likely on a college campus with other middle- and upper-middle-class students. Ultimately, though, the jury is out on whether a national-service requirement would actually promote "virtue and public spiritedness." The choices Americans make to sort themselves along the lines of class, race, and region seem too powerful to be bridled by such a requirement, however well-intentioned. More important, Fukuyama insightfully articulates the challenge identity politics confronts liberal democracies with, especially America. The major flaw in Fukuyama's argument, though, is that it does not adequately acknowledge that liberal democracies remain strong to the degree that they know which identities *not* to recognize.

But in the twenty-first century, the proposals Fukuyama offers are too weak to counteract the atavism and vitalism of identity politics. The main problem is Fukuyama's assumption that America is a creedal nation and should therefore promote a creedal identity. As he puts it: "The creedal national identity that emerged in the wake of the American Civil War today needs to be strongly reemphasized and defended from attacks by both the left and the right."[11] Here he gets it completely wrong. It's no longer enough to appeal to a creedal identity in the way Martin Luther King Jr. and the civil rights movement did. Creedalism is only one part of the American identity, albeit a very important part. The other part of the American identity is cultural. Of course, these two aspects of the American identity are not mutually exclusive. The creedalist's argument is captured eloquently by Abraham Lincoln's Gettysburg Address. His "new birth of freedom"[12] was a call to Americans to ground their collective identity in substantive ideas such as constitutionalism, rule of law, and human equality. All of which, by itself, amounts to a creedal or notional definition of citizenship. However, Lincoln's First Inaugural Address in 1861 also speaks about the "mystic chords of memory."[13] In the address, Lincoln appeals to the very real sentiments that unite Americans as Americans, north and south. The sacrifice made by the Founders, the address reminds us, should be a source of strength and comforts to a beleaguered nation during a time of a national identity crises and political disruption. The principles and way of life animated by the spirit of 1776 is both felt and believed in. Today, we are undergoing a similar period of national identity crisis, and in need of similar chords of memory to unite us as Americans.

Thus, the formation of the American identity does not begin with creedal or notional ideas *only*. It begins in a particular geographic location, among a particular culture, and among a particular people—a core. David Hackett Fischer's *Albion's Seed* convincingly shows that the American identity was formed from a core of English-speaking settlers that settled across the eastern United States from 1629 to 1775. These immigrants and their British folkways account for the various regional cultures that endure today. Americans no longer have a common ancestry, but we certainly have a common culture that goes beyond mere ideas. America consists of a core culture, animated by ideas. It has a civic national and cultural identity. The overriding feature of the core American culture is its Anglo-Protestant disposition: individualism (not excessive nor expressive), moral reform, religiosity, and a robust work ethic. The promotion of this core culture—its values and beliefs—amounts to a "healthy nationalism" of sorts. A healthy nationalism is one that tacks between the Scylla of blood-and-soil nationalism and the Charybdis of feeble notional, creedal, or civic nationalism. As Americans, we have inherited a dual tradition. As the historian Wilfred M. McClay puts it,

> Lincoln's oratory offered two different effects of invoking the mystic chords of memory-first, as reminders of an inherited way of life and, second, as a reminder of a set of universal propositions. This duality is at the heart of a longstanding debate about the nature of American institutions, and indeed it now presents itself at the heart of contemporary debates about multiculturalism, immigration, and national identity.[14]

Identity as Rootedness

Tamir's endorsement of nationalism, and her claim that nationalism is uniquely equipped to encourage a national identity over self-regarding identities based on race, for example, has proven to be provocative in some quarters. But her arguments about nationalism are not provocative at all. Her characterization of nationalism resembles what I refer to above as healthy nationalism. Traditionalist and conservative intellectuals from Aristotle and Joseph de Maistre to Robert Nisbet and Paul Edward Gottfried have all recognized the need for institutional mechanisms besides market forces to unite the disparate parts of a city-state or nation-state. It is important to point out here that, contrary to some on the Right, identity politics is not simply ideological identities in "racial, cultural, or sexual disguise."[15] It is a response to the same market and cultural forces that have fragmented other ascriptive communities in America—family, faith communities, ethnic communities. The overriding question of those who embrace identity politics, ironically, seems to be, "Who am I?" The question is not simply one's personal reflection, but rather it's performative. It demands that one's assumed identity be recognized and should have juridical standing. College campuses are filled with this type of corrosive identity politics. America's ethnically diverse population, and the alienation that some of its members express through oppositional identities, would be well served by what nationalism has to offer.

Tamir offers some version of a healthy type of nationalism, but only partly so. She highlights that conservatives emphasize a shared history and inherited rights and responsibilities in the formation of the nation-state, whereas liberals and progressives emphasize an expressive individualism: the belief that an individual's actions and relationships are freely chosen. Such beliefs make it easy for one to construe one's identity, too, as completely chosen and without any type of social or moral obligation toward one's fellow citizens. This leads one to identify more with members of one's race, or with other sub-national identities, rather than feeling a sense of connectedness with other Americans based on color-blind notions: shared values, norms, and culture. Accordingly, Tamir advocates for the need of public policy to be sensitive to the role of language, religion, and culture in emphasizing a common past and common future among a people.

Likewise, Tamir points out that citizens have a psychological need for membership in a particular place. Particular places imbue their citizens with "thick," as opposed to "thin," identities. Thin identities have weak cultural reference points; they are not grounded in any sort of particularity. Individuals with such identities aspire to be citizens of the world, but instead become citizens of nowhere.[16] Thick identities are formed from the relationships, culture, and norms that each citizen internalizes simply by being American. The initial formation of thick identities begins at the local level of family, neighborhoods, and community, and it is in these particular gatherings that citizens learn to interpret their environment.

It is not only particularity that defines identities. The formation of identity also requires a broad narrative that integrates the particular—home, neighborhood, and community—into a country's national narrative. The simplicity and effectiveness of narratives confer a sense of naturalness on the state and its cultural particularities. National narratives can be construed broadly or narrowly. Alongside broad narratives such as George Washington and the cherry tree or "All Men Are Created Equal," or Lincoln and the log cabin, narrow narratives are communicated by institutions at the local level—through schools, museums, movies, and books—which function to disseminate the national story. National narratives need not be accurate in a strict sense, and they need not be noble lies. To be powerful, national narratives need most of all to appeal to the emotions and the human need to belong to something more than oneself. Just as significant, effective national narratives prevent the growth of antagonistic identities within the body-politic, whereas weak national narratives encourage their growth.

Earlier I said that Tamir offers some version of a healthy type of nationalism, but that she offers it only partly so. My partial endorsement of her version of nationalism is based on her rejection of the non-interference principle of the minimal state that allows its citizens to make the best use of their accumulated human capital for their own benefit. Nationalism as it is conventionally understood does not have to be rooted in blood-and-soil rhetoric and practices to be unifying. It also doesn't have to advocate an active government to be effective. It must hold, however, that the formation of citizens' identities does not begin solely with propositions or creeds. Instead, it begins in a particular geographic location, among a particular culture, and among a particular people.

The Need for a Color-Blind Narrative

In addition to the need for a broad American national identity that's more integrative than self-regarding identities based on race, gender, or religion, we need a positive, compelling American narrative in the public square that's more effective at promoting integration and rootedness. This is the only way to counteract the ever-proliferating anti-color-blind ideas that are tearing us apart, especially so in our institutions of higher education. Narratives are supposed to glue a people together, so to speak. New immigrants to America, for example, exchange their old narratives and identities that once defined them in their old countries for a new, American identity and narrative. But except for learning a few facts about American history and how the government functions, it's not clear at all what narrative or narratives new immigrants to America adopt. Given the feeble patriotism expressed by America's young today, I'm doubtful that whatever narrative new immigrants to America adopt is compelling enough to win their complete allegiance over the long term.[17]

The more positive American narrative would tell a story about the role faith, family, and tradition have played and continue to play in the evolution of the country, both politically and culturally. That story would celebrate what were once widely agreed-upon cultural precepts, also known as the success sequence: that you should, for example, finish high school, get married before having children, and respect the laws. Liberals and progressives have rejected this narrative. What accounts for the Left's negative reaction against those who extol the success sequence is the recognition that conservatives confidently embrace this particular set of values as better than a progressive set of values, at least when it comes to promoting personal fulfillment and societal cohesion. And because the Left is often uncomfortable making value judgments, the perceived judgmentalism on the part of conservatives infuriates the Left. African Americans, too, would greatly benefit from a more positive American narrative that also promotes the success sequence.

As one of the oldest minority groups in America, questions about identity have always been a persistent feature of African American culture. Given the history of African Americans, expressions of black identity have often been at odds with the formation of a positive American narrative. Considering how far they have come culturally, if any group should celebrate the success sequence, it should be African Americans. Take marriage and family. The income gap between married black couples and white married couples is negligible,[18] whereas the income gap between black single parents and white married couples is astronomical. This is to say nothing of the fact that only 37.9 percent of black children, according to the latest dataset in the 2020 Current Population Survey (CPS), live in a married, two parent household. The vast majority of black children are raised in single, female-headed households. Despite the valiant effort single black mothers show in raising their children, they can't be both good mothers and good fathers, and they shouldn't have to be.

As W. Brad Wilcox, Director of the National Marriage Project at the University of Virginia, has documented, the negative psychological and social effects of fatherlessness on black boys have been devastating.[19] The psychological toll can manifest in many destructive ways. Research shows that young black boys have more behavioral problems in the early school years and more delinquency or criminal behavior as adolescents and adults. Some of the anti-color-blind defenders I have discussed in previous chapters teach through their writings and conferences on race that the idea of a two-parent home, the need for fathers and mothers, is a racist construct produced by a powerful white majority. Nothing could be further from the truth. The breakdown of the black family is the root cause of so many of the social ills that confront the black community, black males, and the American community as a *whole*. Given all of this, the success sequence and its timeless color-blind values should be vitally important to the African American community.

CHAPTER 13

Conclusion: Comfortable Racism

T
hroughout this book, I've presented a color-blind racial narrative to counter the one that now predominates in the public square. It's incumbent upon all Americans, especially conservative Americans, to embrace the color-blind narrative before the *comfortable racism* in the guise of Critical Race Theory (CRT), antiracism, and diversity, equity, and inclusion (DEI) seeps even further into the body politic, permanently dividing America against itself.[1] The term *comfortable racism* describes an environment we are slowly growing accustomed to. It results from middle-class exhaustion with the topic of race combined with ideology of antiracism. *Comfortable racism* is separate but equal by choice. It's where our society is heading if my argument for the virtue of color-blindness isn't taken seriously.

It's not enough to offer encouragement *sub rosa* to those who have the courage to speak out against the likes of Kendi and DiAngelo. We must all find our public voices in the fight against their blatantly un-American racial ideas. Those among us who are sympathetic to the color-blind argument, but reluctant to oppose anti-color-blind ideas or policies, usually are so because they know they will be characterized as insensitive to people of color, particularly African Americans. There's also an additional reason for reluctance, which is that in some quarters, professional advancement requires toeing the party line on controversial issues, so it is best to keep one's head down on the topic of race or ethnicity. I hear these sorts of reasons for reluctance from white people a lot. The reluctance from African Americans to speak out against color-conscious ideas or policies is similar to the misgiving expressed by white people, but with the added sensitivity of knowing that they will be ostracized by a vocal segment of the African American community and their white, liberal allies for being a sellout.

Hard though it may be, we can no longer afford to indulge our reluctance to challenge segregationist thinking. Only recently, CRT and antiracism were both fringe ideas limited to ethnic study courses that very few people had heard of or even had an interest in. Slowly but surely, though, both ideologies moved methodically to the center of mainstream discussions of race on the heels of several racial upheavals. For CRT it was the O. J. Simpson case and the push for jury nullification on racial grounds. The event that moved antiracism to the center of mainstream discussions of race was the death of George Floyd. CRT and antiracism are opportunistic ideologies wielded by opportunistic individuals who have no interest in seeing America flourish as a multiracial democratic republic. So moving forward, as color-blind Americans, we must all speak up in our school classrooms, places of worship, and in our places of employment against ways of thinking that divide us along racial and ethnic lines. If we have to call our child's school to challenge the assignment that demonizes white people as victimizers, or the assignment that characterizes patriotic African Americans as racially confused, do it! We must do our part to stand up to the racial bullying. When reasonable voices are attacked on college campuses for daring to see people of color as individuals, and not as bearers of racial trauma in need of safe spaces and separate graduations, we must fight back. We cannot return to a racially complacent mindset, where people look the other way out of cowardice, to go along to get along. We cannot let the doctrine of separate but equal creep back into American life.

Recently, my daughter wrote a high school research paper about the Scottsboro boys. This infamous, heartbreaking case was about nine African American boys who were abused, manipulated, and jailed illegally for having been accused, falsely, of rape near Scottsboro, Alabama in 1931. The country was outraged by the treatment of the boys. Harper Lee's novel *To Kill a Mockingbird* is based, in part, on some of the racial themes highlighted in the Scottsboro Case. The case was instrumental in building momentum for the civil rights movement. My point is that to be color-blind isn't to be ignorant of America's racial past. It's the ability to not be defined by our racial past, as individuals and as a country. This is what I reminded my daughter as she wrote about the Scottsboro case. We can't allow ourselves as Americans to resegregate along the lines of race today, by choice. There is a big difference between those who want racial harmony and equality, and those who believe racism is natural. We must take a stand against conflating these two claims by embracing the only viable position worth taking in a heterogeneous society such as ours: the color-blind position.

Much of what motivates the opposition to color-blind principles is white guilt. A common theme in DiAngelo is a generalized discomfort with race expressed by whites and, more specifically, white liberals. Given our racial past, some of the discomfort is understandable. However, the antiracist teachings aren't dealing with this discomfort in good faith. The antiracist crowd is capitalizing on America's racial insecurities and exploiting it to amass influence across key sectors of society, and to sow division among us, especially our young. The diversity trainers preach to us that their goal is to "just have a conversation" on race. But their real goal is to create anger, separation, and enemies among the American people.

To be an antiracist is to want to destroy completely the ordered liberty that has defined our way of life for nearly three hundred years. Some among us, sadly, have been won over by these racist ideologies and convinced to believe that to be color-conscious is the new normal, the way forward. Listen to the actual words of Bell, Kendi, Coates, DiAngelo, and many others who are part of the woke movement. When they argue that white people need to hear the pain and feel the trauma undergone by African Americans, what they are really saying is that white people need to hear the pain and then sacrifice themselves many times over. According to this way of thinking, whites will never redeem themselves, change, grow, or be forgiven for their forebears' deeds. As I write these words, a California commission set up by Governor Newsom has passed a resolution to make a formal apology to the African Americans residents in the state by giving them reparations for slavery. It's an attempt to move past the shadow of slavery. However, everyone knows that this latest move in the reparations gambit isn't an attempt to bring Californians together with a lasting monetary acknowledgment of slavery. There is nothing of the sort mentioned. Why? Because victimology has a goal, and only one goal, and that is to be a victim forever. The goalpost will continue to move, racial spoils will accumulate, unless Americans committed to equality and color-blind principles take a stand and say enough is enough.

Martin Luther King Jr. took a stand; he was not a victim. Frederick Douglass took a stand. They were both Christian men who lived according to their faith's moral standards. King and Douglass fought for racial harmony, and there is no common ground whatsoever between antiracism and King's or Douglass's vision. You cannot follow Kendi's teachings and at the same time praise King's message. Both King and Douglass believed that racism is unnatural, destructive, and must not be accepted—this is the color-blind standard. Color-blindness is about how we treat others, and as I have pointed out, it's not about denying hardship. It embraces hardship so that we can learn to be better Americans, to listen to our better angels as a people. Antiracism, on the other hand, capitalizes on yesterday's hardships and subjects whites to continuous flagellation.

We cannot afford to go along with the pernicious CRT, antiracism message because of white guilt. Imagine if we all settle into a sort of comfortable racism. Out of exhaustion, we say, "Okay, let's just let the antiracists be—at least the kids will learn something about the pain from our past." This is naïve thinking. Having separate but equal by choice is not what thousands of black and white Americans lost their lives fighting for during the journey up from slavery and out of Jim Crow. They fought to be judged by the content of their character, not by the color of their skin. Conservatives—all Americans—must stand against the vile doctrine of separate but equal, whatever form it might take.

Acknowledgments

First and foremost, I must thank my wife, Eleanora, for her unwavering support throughout the process of writing this book. We have been married twenty-five years, and during that time my wife has always embodied the very idea of color-blindness. The many discussions we have had on the topic over the years have resulted in her establishing the "Archie family philosophy." It is the belief that children should be raised from the inside out, which means the development of a child's moral character must be prioritized over the other ever present superficial demands on a child's identity. My wife's intellectual support and the motivation it has provided me have made all the difference in who I am today. She's my number one intellectual partner. I'm truly blessed to have such a kindhearted, smart, and supportive wife, who is also a loving mother to our three children. She truly has been the wind beneath all of our wings.

Speaking of my children, there's nothing like one's own children to remind parents to practice what we preach. My children often reminded me not to procrastinate and to sit down and write. It was that simple for them. Well, I finally did! With love to my wonderful children, you guys helped push me over the finish line.

In writing this book, I have tried to offer a way forward out of the morass of race and the way Americans discuss race. The only plausible way forward in a heterogenous society like the United States of America resides in the commitment to color-blind principles at the individual level and at the institutional level. For me, my mother's commitment to these principles was decisive. She did her best to make sure the environments we frequented as children were integrated, fair, and open, so I would like to acknowledge, with love and honor, my mother, Shirley.

There are several people who have proved instrumental in giving me the opportunity early on to express my ideas in "public facing" settings, which ultimately led to the book you have before you. Daniel McCarthy, current editor of the conservative academic journal *Modern Age*, has certainly been instrumental in this respect.

Daniel was always encouraging and open to various book review pitches I sent his way back when he was editor of the *American Conservative* (TAC). When Daniel assumed the editorship of *Modern Age*, I continued to write reviews for him there. Ultimately, it was Dan who introduced me to the wonderful team at Regnery. Dan is the ideal editor: thorough, kind, encouraging, and smart. Aside from his skill set as editor, I have learned a lot from Dan about the vital role conservatism must play in reforming contemporary culture, especially as it relates to identity politics. I am thankful for the support and opportunities you have extended to me. I hope our paths continue to cross. Thank you!

In addition to the *American Conservative* and *Modern Age*, *National Review*, under the editorship of Rich Lowry, has provided a forum in its pages for me to express some of the views contained in this book. He has always been willing to take my calls and offer advice on various writerly-related issues. Thanks for the encouragement and continued support, Rich.

Over the last several years, Yoram Hazony has kindly invited me to speak at the NatCon conferences, where I was given the opportunity to work through my thesis of color-blindness in a setting of sharp minds, conservative voices, and patriotic Americans. Prior to my first attendance at NatCon in 2019, I was not familiar with Yoram nor his NatCon movement. Since that time, I have learned many positive things from both, some of which are contained in chapter 12. I extend a special thanks to you, Yoram.

Most important, I owe a big "thank you" to those at Regnery who found my ideas compelling enough to put them inside of a book. This is all the more significant because the book is published with the nation's premier conservative publisher. I am grateful for all the help Regnery has provided in ushering the book to completeness. I owe a special thanks to Tom Spence, Harry Crocker, Tony Daniel, and Michael Baker. And a thanks to John Caruso for taking the time to help me decide on which dingbats to use.

Last but not least, this book was made possible in no small part through funding provided by the Department of Philosophy at Colorado State University. I am very thankful for my Department's support and its consistent commitment to intellectual diversity.

Appendix A

As mentioned in Frederick Douglass's My Bondage and My Freedom, *the short dialogue below between a master and his slave "powerfully affected" the young enslaved Douglass and reinforced his love of liberty.*

Caleb Bingham, editor. *"Dialogue between a Master and Slave."* The Columbian Orator. *Boston: Manning & Loring, 1797, 240–42.*

Master.
NOW, villain! what have you to say for this second attempt to run away? Is there any punishment that you do not deserve?
Slave.
I well know that nothing I can say will avail. I submit to my fate.
Mast.
But are you not a base fellow, a hardened and ungrateful rascal?
Slave.
I am a slave. That is answer enough.

Mast.

I am not content with that answer. I thought I discerned in you some tokens of a mind superior to your condition. I treated you accordingly. You have been comfortably fed and lodged, not over-worked, and attended with the most humane care when you were sick. And is this the return?

Slave.

Since you condescend to talk with me, as man to man, I will reply. What have you done, what can you do for me, that will compensate for the liberty which you have taken away?

Mast.

I did not take it away. You were a slave when I fairly purchased you.

Slave.

Did I give my consent to the purchase?

Mast.

You had no consent to give. You had already lost the right of disposing of yourself.

Slave.

I had lost the power, but how the right? I was treacherously kid-napped in my own country, when following an honest occupation. I was put in chains, sold to one of your countrymen, carried by force on board his ship, brought hither, and exposed to sale like a beast in the market, where you bought me. What step in all this progress of violence and injustice can give a right? Was it in the villain who stole me, in the slave-merchant who tempted him to do so, or in you who encouraged the slave-merchant to bring his cargo of human cattle to cultivate your lands?

Mast.

It is in the order of Providence that one man should become subservient to another. It ever has been so, and ever will be. I found the custom, and did not make it.

Slave.

You cannot but be sensible, that the robber who puts a pistol to your breast may make just the same plea. Providence gives him a power over your life and property; it gave my enemies a power over my liberty. But it has also given me legs to escape with; and what should prevent me from using them? Nay, what should restrain me from retaliating the wrongs I have suffered, if a favorable occasion should offer?

Mast.

Gratitude; I repeat, gratitude! Have I not endeavored ever since I possessed you to alleviate your misfortunes by kind treatment; and does that confer no obligation? Consider how much worse your condition might have been under another master.

Slave.

You have done nothing for me more than for your working cattle. Are they not well fed and tended? do you work them harder than your slaves? is not the rule of treating both designed only for your own advantage? You treat both your men and beast slaves better than some of your neighbors, because you are more prudent and wealthy than they.

Mast.

You might add, more humane too.

Slave.

Humane! Does it deserve that appellation to keep your fellow-men in forced subjection, deprived of all exercise of their free will, liable to all the injuries that your own caprice, or the brutality of your overseers, may heap on them, and devoted, soul and body, only to your pleasure and emolument? Can gratitude take place between creatures in such a state, and the tyrant who holds them in it? Look at these limbs; are they not those of a man? Think that I have the spirit of a man too.

Mast.

But it was my intention not only to make your life tolerably comfortable at present, but to provide for you in your old age.

Slave.

Alas! is a life like mine, torn from country, friends, and all I held dear, and compelled to toil under the burning sun for a master, worth thinking about for old age? No; the sooner it ends, the sooner I shall obtain that relief for which my soul pants.

Mast.

Is it impossible, then, to hold you by any ties but those of constraint and severity?

Slave.

It is impossible to make one, who has felt the value of freedom, acquiesce in being a slave.

Mast.

Suppose I were to restore you to your liberty, would you reckon that a favor?

Slave.

The greatest: for although it would only be undoing a wrong, I know too well how few among mankind are capable of sacrificing interest to justice, not to prize the exertion when it is made.

Mast.

I do it, then; be free.

Slave.

Now I am indeed your servant, though not your slave. And as the first return I can make for your kindness, I will tell you freely the condition in which you live. You are surrounded with implacable foes, who long for a safe opportunity to revenge upon you and the other planters all the miseries they have endured. The more generous their natures, the more indignant they feel against that cruel injustice which has dragged them hither, and doomed them to perpetual servitude. You can rely on no kindness on your parts to soften the obduracy of their resentment. You have reduced them to the state of brute beasts; and if they have not the stupidity of beasts of burden, they must have the ferocity of beasts of prey. Superior force alone can give you security. As soon as that fails, you are at the mercy of the merciless. Such is the social bond between master and slave!

Appendix B

The Declaration of Independence

IN CONGRESS, July 4, 1776.

The unanimous Declaration of the thirteen united States of America,

When in the Course of human events, it becomes necessary for one people to dissolve the political bands which have connected them with another, and to assume among the powers of the earth, the separate and equal station to which the Laws of Nature and of Nature's God entitle them, a decent respect to the opinions of mankind requires that they should declare the causes which impel them to the separation.

We hold these truths to be self-evident, that all men are created equal, that they are endowed by their Creator with certain unalienable Rights, that among these are Life, Liberty and the pursuit of Happiness.– That to secure these rights, Governments are instituted among Men, deriving their just powers from the consent of the governed, –That whenever any Form of Government becomes destructive of these ends, it is the Right of the People to alter or to abolish it, and to institute new

Government, laying its foundation on such principles and organizing its powers in such form, as to them shall seem most likely to effect their Safety and Happiness. Prudence, indeed, will dictate that Governments long established should not be changed for light and transient causes; and accordingly all experience hath shewn, that mankind are more disposed to suffer, while evils are sufferable, than to right themselves by abolishing the forms to which they are accustomed. But when a long train of abuses and usurpations, pursuing invariably the same Object evinces a design to reduce them under absolute Despotism, it is their right, it is their duty, to throw off such Government, and to provide new Guards for their future security.–Such has been the patient sufferance of these Colonies; and such is now the necessity which constrains them to alter their former Systems of Government. The history of the present King of Great Britain is a history of repeated injuries and usurpations, all having in direct object the establishment of an absolute Tyranny over these States. To prove this, let Facts be submitted to a candid world.

He has refused his Assent to Laws, the most wholesome and necessary for the public good.

He has forbidden his Governors to pass Laws of immediate and pressing importance, unless suspended in their operation till his Assent should be obtained; and when so suspended, he has utterly neglected to attend to them.

He has refused to pass other Laws for the accommodation of large districts of people, unless those people would relinquish the right of Representation in the Legislature, a right inestimable to them and formidable to tyrants only.

He has called together legislative bodies at places unusual, uncomfortable, and distant from the depository of their public Records, for the sole purpose of fatiguing them into compliance with his measures.

He has dissolved Representative Houses repeatedly, for opposing with manly firmness his invasions on the rights of the people.

He has refused for a long time, after such dissolutions, to cause others to be elected; whereby the Legislative powers, incapable of Annihilation, have returned to the People at large for their exercise; the State remaining in the mean time exposed to all the dangers of invasion from without, and convulsions within.

He has endeavoured to prevent the population of these States; for that purpose obstructing the Laws for Naturalization of Foreigners; refusing to pass others to encourage their migrations hither, and raising the conditions of new Appropriations of Lands.

He has obstructed the Administration of Justice, by refusing his Assent to Laws for establishing Judiciary powers.

He has made Judges dependent on his Will alone, for the tenure of their offices, and the amount and payment of their salaries.

He has erected a multitude of New Offices, and sent hither swarms of Officers to harrass our people, and eat out their substance.

He has kept among us, in times of peace, Standing Armies without the Consent of our legislatures.

He has affected to render the Military independent of and superior to the Civil power.

He has combined with others to subject us to a jurisdiction foreign to our constitution, and unacknowledged by our laws; giving his Assent to their Acts of pretended Legislation:

For Quartering large bodies of armed troops among us:

For protecting them, by a mock Trial, from punishment for any Murders which they should commit on the Inhabitants of these States:

For cutting off our Trade with all parts of the world:

For imposing Taxes on us without our Consent:

For depriving us in many cases, of the benefits of Trial by Jury:

For transporting us beyond Seas to be tried for pretended offences

For abolishing the free System of English Laws in a neighbouring Province, establishing therein an Arbitrary government, and enlarging its Boundaries so as to render it at once an example and fit instrument for introducing the same absolute rule into these Colonies:

For taking away our Charters, abolishing our most valuable Laws, and altering fundamentally the Forms of our Governments:

For suspending our own Legislatures, and declaring themselves invested with power to legislate for us in all cases whatsoever.

He has abdicated Government here, by declaring us out of his Protection and waging War against us.

He has plundered our seas, ravaged our Coasts, burnt our towns, and destroyed the lives of our people.

He is at this time transporting large Armies of foreign Mercenaries to compleat the works of death, desolation and tyranny, already begun with circumstances of Cruelty & perfidy scarcely paralleled in the most barbarous ages, and totally unworthy the Head of a civilized nation.

He has constrained our fellow Citizens taken Captive on the high Seas to bear Arms against their Country, to become the executioners of their friends and Brethren, or to fall themselves by their Hands.

He has excited domestic insurrections amongst us, and has endeavoured to bring on the inhabitants of our frontiers, the merciless Indian Savages, whose known rule of warfare, is an undistinguished destruction of all ages, sexes and conditions.

In every stage of these Oppressions We have Petitioned for Redress in the most humble terms: Our repeated Petitions have been answered only by repeated injury. A Prince whose character is thus marked by every act which may define a Tyrant, is unfit to be the ruler of a free people.

Nor have We been wanting in attentions to our Brittish brethren. We have warned them from time to time of attempts by their legislature to extend an unwarrantable jurisdiction over us. We have reminded them of the circumstances of our emigration and settlement here. We have appealed to their native justice and magnanimity, and we have conjured them by the ties of our common kindred to disavow these usurpations, which, would inevitably interrupt our connections and correspondence. They too have been deaf to the voice of justice and of consanguinity. We must, therefore, acquiesce in the necessity, which denounces our Separation, and hold them, as we hold the rest of mankind, Enemies in War, in Peace Friends.

We, therefore, the Representatives of the united States of America, in General Congress, Assembled, appealing to the Supreme Judge of the world for the rectitude of our intentions, do, in the Name, and by Authority of the good People of these Colonies, solemnly publish and declare, That these United Colonies are, and of Right ought to be Free and Independent States; that they are Absolved from all Allegiance to the British Crown, and that all political connection between them and the State of Great Britain, is and ought to be totally dissolved; and that as Free and Independent States, they have full Power to levy War, conclude Peace, contract Alliances, establish Commerce, and to do all other Acts and Things which Independent States may of right do. And for the support of this Declaration, with a firm reliance on the protection of divine Providence, we mutually pledge to each other our Lives, our Fortunes and our sacred Honor.

Georgia
Button Gwinnett, Lyman Hall, George Walton

North Carolina
William Hooper, Joseph Hewes, John Penn

South Carolina
Edward Rutledge, Thomas Heyward, Jr., Thomas Lynch, Jr., Arthur Middleton

Massachusetts
John Hancock

Maryland
Samuel Chase, William Paca, Thomas Stone, Charles Carroll of Carrollton

Virginia
George Wythe, Richard Henry Lee, Thomas Jefferson, Benjamin Harrison, Thomas Nelson, Jr., Francis Lightfoot Lee, Carter Braxton

Pennsylvania
Robert Morris, Benjamin Rush, Benjamin Franklin, John Morton, George Clymer, James Smith, George Taylor, James Wilson, George Ross

Delaware
Caesar Rodney, George Read, Thomas McKean

New York
William Floyd, Philip Livingston, Francis Lewis, Lewis Morris

New Jersey
Richard Stockton, John Witherspoon, Francis Hopkinson, John Hart, Abraham Clark

New Hampshire
Josiah Bartlett, William Whipple

Massachusetts
Samuel Adams, John Adams, Robert Treat Paine, Elbridge Gerry

Rhode Island:
Stephen Hopkins, William Ellery

Connecticut
Roger Sherman, Samuel Huntington, William Williams, Oliver Wolcott

New Hampshire
Matthew Thornton

Appendix C

The Constitution of the United States of America

We the People of the United States, in Order to form a more perfect Union, establish Justice, insure domestic Tranquility, provide for the common defence, promote the general Welfare, and secure the Blessings of Liberty to ourselves and our Posterity, do ordain and establish this Constitution for the United States of America.

The Constitutional Convention

Article I

Section 1: Congress

All legislative Powers herein granted shall be vested in a Congress of the United States, which shall consist of a Senate and House of Representatives.

Section 2: The House of Representatives

The House of Representatives shall be composed of Members chosen every second Year by the People of the several States, and the Electors in each State shall have the Qualifications requisite for Electors of the most numerous Branch of the State Legislature.

No Person shall be a Representative who shall not have attained to the Age of twenty five Years, and been seven Years a Citizen of the United States, and who shall not, when elected, be an Inhabitant of that State in which he shall be chosen.

Representatives and direct Taxes shall be apportioned among the several States which may be included within this Union, according to their respective Numbers, which shall be determined by adding to the whole Number of free Persons, including those bound to Service for a Term of Years, and excluding Indians not taxed, three fifths of all other Persons. The actual Enumeration shall be made within three Years after the first Meeting of the Congress of the United States, and within every subsequent Term of ten Years, in such Manner as they shall by Law direct. The number of Representatives shall not exceed one for every thirty Thousand, but each State shall have at Least one Representative; and until such enumeration shall be made, the State of New Hampshire shall be entitled to chuse three, Massachusetts eight, Rhode-Island and Providence Plantations one, Connecticut five, New-York six, New Jersey four, Pennsylvania eight, Delaware one, Maryland six, Virginia ten, North Carolina five, South Carolina five, and Georgia three.

When vacancies happen in the Representation from any State, the Executive Authority thereof shall issue Writs of Election to fill such Vacancies.

The House of Representatives shall chuse their Speaker and other Officers; and shall have the sole Power of Impeachment.

Section 3: The Senate

The Senate of the United States shall be composed of two Senators from each State, chosen by the Legislature thereof, for six Years; and each Senator shall have one Vote.

Immediately after they shall be assembled in Consequence of the first Election, they shall be divided as equally as may be into three Classes. The Seats of the Senators of the first Class shall be vacated at the Expiration of the second Year, of the second Class at the Expiration of the fourth Year, and of the third Class at the Expiration of the sixth Year, so that one third may be chosen every second Year; and if Vacancies happen by Resignation, or otherwise, during the Recess of the Legislature of any State, the Executive thereof may make temporary Appointments until the next Meeting of the Legislature, which shall then fill such Vacancies.

No Person shall be a Senator who shall not have attained to the Age of thirty Years, and been nine Years a Citizen of the United States, and who shall not, when elected, be an Inhabitant of that State for which he shall be chosen.

The Vice President of the United States shall be President of the Senate, but shall have no Vote, unless they be equally divided.

The Senate shall chuse their other Officers, and also a President pro tempore, in the Absence of the Vice President, or when he shall exercise the Office of President of the United States.

The Senate shall have the sole Power to try all Impeachments. When sitting for that Purpose, they shall be on Oath or Affirmation. When the President of the United States is tried, the Chief Justice shall preside: And no Person shall be convicted without the Concurrence of two thirds of the Members present.

Judgment in Cases of Impeachment shall not extend further than to removal from Office, and disqualification to hold and enjoy any

Office of honor, Trust or Profit under the United States: but the Party convicted shall nevertheless be liable and subject to Indictment, Trial, Judgment and Punishment, according to Law.

Section 4: Elections

The Times, Places and Manner of holding Elections for Senators and Representatives, shall be prescribed in each State by the Legislature thereof; but the Congress may at any time by Law make or alter such Regulations, except as to the Places of chusing Senators.

The Congress shall assemble at least once in every Year, and such Meeting shall be on the first Monday in December, unless they shall by Law appoint a different Day.

Section 5: Powers and Duties of Congress

Each House shall be the Judge of the Elections, Returns and Qualifications of its own Members, and a Majority of each shall constitute a Quorum to do Business; but a smaller Number may adjourn from day to day, and may be authorized to compel the Attendance of absent Members, in such Manner, and under such Penalties as each House may provide.

Each House may determine the Rules of its Proceedings, punish its Members for disorderly Behaviour, and, with the Concurrence of two thirds, expel a Member.

Each House shall keep a Journal of its Proceedings, and from time to time publish the same, excepting such Parts as may in their Judgment require Secrecy; and the Yeas and Nays of the Members of either House on any question shall, at the Desire of one fifth of those Present, be entered on the Journal.

Neither House, during the Session of Congress, shall, without the Consent of the other, adjourn for more than three days, nor to any other Place than that in which the two Houses shall be sitting.

Section 6: Rights and Disabilities of Members

The Senators and Representatives shall receive a Compensation for their Services, to be ascertained by Law, and paid out of the Treasury of the United States. They shall in all Cases, except Treason, Felony and Breach of the Peace, be privileged from Arrest during their Attendance at the Session of their respective Houses, and in going to and returning from the same; and for any Speech or Debate in either House, they shall not be questioned in any other Place.

No Senator or Representative shall, during the Time for which he was elected, be appointed to any civil Office under the Authority of the United States, which shall have been created, or the Emoluments whereof shall have been encreased during such time; and no Person holding any Office under the United States, shall be a Member of either House during his Continuance in Office.

Section 7: Legislative Process

All Bills for raising Revenue shall originate in the House of Representatives; but the Senate may propose or concur with Amendments as on other Bills.

Every Bill which shall have passed the House of Representatives and the Senate, shall, before it become a Law, be presented to the President of the United States; If he approve he shall sign it, but if not he shall return it, with his Objections to that House in which it shall have originated, who shall enter the Objections at large on their Journal, and proceed to reconsider it. If after such Reconsideration two thirds of that House shall agree to pass the Bill, it shall be sent, together with the Objections, to the other House, by which it shall likewise be reconsidered, and if approved by two thirds of that House, it shall become a Law. But in all such Cases the Votes of both Houses shall be determined by Yeas and Nays, and the Names of the Persons voting for and against the Bill shall be entered on the Journal of each House respectively. If any Bill shall not be returned by the President within ten Days (Sundays excepted) after it shall have been presented to him, the Same shall be a Law, in like Manner as if he had signed it, unless the Congress by their Adjournment prevent its Return, in which Case it shall not be a Law.

Every Order, Resolution, or Vote to which the Concurrence of the Senate and House of Representatives may be necessary (except on a question of Adjournment) shall be presented to the President of the United States; and before the Same shall take Effect, shall be approved by him, or being disapproved by him, shall be repassed by two thirds of the Senate and House of Representatives, according to the Rules and Limitations prescribed in the Case of a Bill.

Section 8: Powers of Congress

The Congress shall have Power To lay and collect Taxes, Duties, Imposts and Excises, to pay the Debts and provide for the common Defence and general Welfare of the United States; but all Duties, Imposts and Excises shall be uniform throughout the United States;

To borrow Money on the credit of the United States;

To regulate Commerce with foreign Nations, and among the several States, and with the Indian Tribes;

To establish a uniform Rule of Naturalization, and uniform Laws on the subject of Bankruptcies throughout the United States;

To coin Money, regulate the Value thereof, and of foreign Coin, and fix the Standard of Weights and Measures;

To provide for the Punishment of counterfeiting the Securities and current Coin of the United States;

To establish Post Offices and post Roads;

To promote the Progress of Science and useful Arts, by securing for limited Times to Authors and Inventors the exclusive Right to their respective Writings and Discoveries;

To constitute Tribunals inferior to the supreme Court;

To define and punish Piracies and Felonies committed on the high Seas, and Offenses against the Law of Nations;

To declare War, grant Letters of Marque and Reprisal, and make Rules concerning Captures on Land and Water;

To raise and support Armies, but no Appropriation of Money to that Use shall be for a longer Term than two Years;

To provide and maintain a Navy;

To make Rules for the Government and Regulation of the land and naval Forces;

To provide for calling forth the Militia to execute the Laws of the Union, suppress Insurrections and repel Invasions;

To provide for organizing, arming, and disciplining, the Militia, and for governing such Part of them as may be employed in the Service of the United States, reserving to the States respectively, the Appointment of the Officers, and the Authority of training the Militia according to the discipline prescribed by Congress;

To exercise exclusive Legislation in all Cases whatsoever, over such District (not exceeding ten Miles square) as may, by Cession of particular States, and the Acceptance of Congress, become the Seat of the Government of the United States, and to exercise like Authority over all Places purchased by the Consent of the

Legislature of the State in which the Same shall be, for the Erection of Forts, Magazines, Arsenals, dock-Yards and other needful Buildings;-And

To make all Laws which shall be necessary and proper for carrying into Execution the foregoing Powers, and all other Powers vested by this Constitution in the Government of the United States, or in any Department or Officer thereof.

Section 9: Powers Denied Congress

The Migration or Importation of such Persons as any of the States now existing shall think proper to admit, shall not be prohibited by the Congress prior to the Year one thousand eight hundred and eight, but a Tax or duty may be imposed on such Importation, not exceeding ten dollars for each Person.

The Privilege of the Writ of Habeas Corpus shall not be suspended, unless when in Cases of Rebellion or Invasion the public Safety may require it.

No Bill of Attainder or ex post facto Law shall be passed.

No Capitation, or other direct, Tax shall be laid, unless in Proportion to the Census or Enumeration herein before directed to be taken.

No Tax or Duty shall be laid on Articles exported from any State.

No Preference shall be given by any Regulation of Commerce or Revenue to the Ports of one State over those of another: nor shall Vessels bound to, or from, one State, be obliged to enter, clear, or pay Duties in another.

No Money shall be drawn from the Treasury, but in Consequence of Appropriations made by Law; and a regular Statement and Account of the Receipts and Expenditures of all public Money shall be published from time to time.

No Title of Nobility shall be granted by the United States: And no Person holding any Office of Profit or Trust under them, shall, without the Consent of the Congress, accept of any present, Emolument, Office, or Title, of any kind whatever, from any King, Prince, or foreign State.

Section 10: Powers Denied to the States

No State shall enter into any Treaty, Alliance, or Confederation; grant Letters of Marque and Reprisal; coin Money; emit Bills of Credit; make any Thing but gold and silver Coin a Tender in Payment of Debts; pass any Bill of Attainder, ex post facto Law, or Law impairing the Obligation of Contracts, or grant any Title of Nobility.

No State shall, without the Consent of the Congress, lay any Imposts or Duties on Imports or Exports, except what may be absolutely necessary for executing it's inspection Laws: and the net Produce of all Duties and Imposts, laid by any State on Imports or Exports, shall be for the Use of the Treasury of the United States; and all such Laws shall be subject to the Revision and Controul of the Congress.

No State shall, without the Consent of Congress, lay any Duty of Tonnage, keep Troops, or Ships of War in time of Peace, enter into any Agreement or Compact with another State, or with a foreign Power, or engage in War, unless actually invaded, or in such imminent Danger as will not admit of delay.

Article II

Section 1

The executive Power shall be vested in a President of the United States of America.

He shall hold his Office during the Term of four Years, and, together with the Vice President, chosen for the same Term, be elected, as follows:

Each State shall appoint, in such Manner as the Legislature thereof may direct, a Number of Electors, equal to the whole Number of Senators and Representatives to which the State may be entitled in the Congress: but no Senator or Representative, or Person holding an Office of Trust or Profit under the United States, shall be appointed an Elector.

The Electors shall meet in their respective States, and vote by Ballot for two Persons, of whom one at least shall not be an Inhabitant of the same State with themselves. And they shall make a List of all the Persons voted for, and of the Number of Votes for each; which List they shall sign and certify, and transmit sealed to the Seat of the Government of the United States, directed to the President of the Senate. The President of the Senate shall, in the Presence of the Senate and House of Representatives, open all the Certificates, and the Votes shall then be counted. The Person having the greatest Number of Votes shall be the President, if such Number be a Majority of the whole Number of Electors appointed; and if there be more than one who have such Majority, and have an equal Number of Votes, then the House of Representatives shall immediately chuse by Ballot one of them for President; and if no Person have a Majority, then from the five highest on the List the said House shall in like Manner chuse the President. But in chusing the President, the Votes shall be taken by States, the Representation from each State having one Vote; A quorum for this Purpose shall consist of a Member or Members from two thirds of the States, and a Majority of all the States shall be necessary to a Choice. In every Case, after the Choice of the President, the Person having the greatest Number of Votes of the Electors shall be the Vice President. But if there should remain two or more who have equal Votes, the Senate shall chuse from them by Ballot the Vice President.

The Congress may determine the Time of chusing the Electors, and the Day on which they shall give their Votes; which Day shall be the same throughout the United States.

No Person except a natural born Citizen, or a Citizen of the United States, at the time of the Adoption of this Constitution, shall be eligible to the Office of President; neither shall any person be eligible to that Office who shall not have attained to the Age of thirty five Years, and been fourteen Years a Resident within the United States.

In Case of the Removal of the President from Office, or of his Death, Resignation, or Inability to discharge the Powers and Duties of the said Office, the Same shall devolve on the Vice President, and the Congress may by Law provide for the Case of Removal, Death, Resignation or Inability, both of the President and Vice President, declaring what Officer shall then act as President, and such Officer shall act accordingly, until the Disability be removed, or a President shall be elected.

The President shall, at stated Times, receive for his Services, a Compensation, which shall neither be increased nor diminished during the Period for which he shall have been elected, and he shall not receive within that Period any other Emolument from the United States, or any of them.

Before he enter on the Execution of his Office, he shall take the following Oath or Affirmation:—"I do solemnly swear (or affirm) that I will faithfully execute the Office of President of the United States, and will to the best of my Ability, preserve, protect and defend the Constitution of the United States."

Section 2

The President shall be Commander in Chief of the Army and Navy of the United States, and of the Militia of the several States, when called into the actual Service of the United States; he may require the Opinion, in writing, of the principal Officer in each of the executive Departments, upon any Subject relating to the Duties of their respective Offices, and he shall have Power to grant Reprieves and Pardons for Offenses against the United States, except in Cases of Impeachment.

He shall have Power, by and with the Advice and Consent of the Senate, to make Treaties, provided two thirds of the Senators present concur; and he shall nominate, and by and with the Advice and Consent of the Senate, shall appoint Ambassadors, other public Ministers and Consuls, Judges of the supreme Court, and all other Officers of the United States, whose Appointments are not herein otherwise provided for, and which shall be established by Law: but the Congress may by Law vest the Appointment of such inferior Officers, as they think proper, in the President alone, in the Courts of Law, or in the Heads of Departments.

The President shall have Power to fill up all Vacancies that may happen during the Recess of the Senate, by granting Commissions which shall expire at the End of their next Session.

Section 3

He shall from time to time give to the Congress Information of the State of the Union, and recommend to their Consideration such Measures as he shall judge necessary and expedient; he may, on extraordinary Occasions, convene both Houses, or either of them, and in Case of Disagreement between them, with Respect to the Time of Adjournment, he may adjourn them to such Time as he shall think proper; he shall receive Ambassadors and other public Ministers; he shall take Care that the Laws be faithfully executed, and shall Commission all the Officers of the United States.

Section 4

The President, Vice President and all civil Officers of the United States, shall be removed from Office on Impeachment for, and Conviction of, Treason, Bribery, or other high Crimes and Misdemeanors.

Article III

Section 1

The judicial Power of the United States, shall be vested in one supreme Court, and in such inferior Courts as the Congress may from time to time ordain and establish. The Judges, both of the supreme and inferior Courts, shall hold their Offices during good Behaviour, and shall, at stated Times, receive for their Services, a Compensation, which shall not be diminished during their Continuance in Office.

Section 2

The judicial Power shall extend to all Cases, in Law and Equity, arising under this Constitution, the Laws of the United States, and Treaties made, or which shall be made, under their Authority;—to all Cases affecting Ambassadors, other public Ministers and Consuls;—to all Cases of admiralty and maritime Jurisdiction;—to Controversies to which the United States shall be a Party;—to Controversies between two or more States;—between a State and Citizens of another State;—between Citizens of different States;—between Citizens of the same State claiming Lands under Grants of different States, and between a State, or the Citizens thereof, and foreign States, Citizens or Subjects.

In all Cases affecting Ambassadors, other public Ministers and Consuls, and those in which a State shall be Party, the supreme Court shall have original Jurisdiction. In all the other Cases before mentioned, the supreme Court shall have appellate Jurisdiction, both as to Law and Fact, with such Exceptions, and under such Regulations as the Congress shall make.

The Trial of all Crimes, except in Cases of Impeachment; shall be by Jury; and such Trial shall be held in the State where the said Crimes shall have been committed; but when not committed within any State, the Trial shall be at such Place or Places as the Congress may by Law have directed.

Section 3

Treason against the United States, shall consist only in levying War against them, or in adhering to their Enemies, giving them Aid and Comfort. No Person shall be convicted of Treason unless on the Testimony of two Witnesses to the same overt Act, or on Confession in open Court.

The Congress shall have Power to declare the Punishment of Treason, but no Attainder of Treason shall work Corruption of Blood, or Forfeiture except during the Life of the Person attainted.

Article IV

Section 1

Full Faith and Credit shall be given in each State to the public Acts, Records, and judicial Proceedings of every other State. And the

Congress may by general Laws prescribe the Manner in which such Acts, Records and Proceedings shall be proved, and the Effect thereof.

Section 2

The Citizens of each State shall be entitled to all Privileges and Immunities of Citizens in the several States.

A Person charged in any State with Treason, Felony, or other Crime, who shall flee from Justice, and be found in another State, shall on Demand of the executive Authority of the State from which he fled, be delivered up, to be removed to the State having Jurisdiction of the Crime.

No Person held to Service or Labour in one State, under the Laws thereof, escaping into another, shall, in Consequence of any Law or Regulation therein, be discharged from such Service or Labour, but shall be delivered up on Claim of the Party to whom such Service or Labour may be due.

Section 3

New States may be admitted by the Congress into this Union; but no new State shall be formed or erected within the Jurisdiction of any other State; nor any State be formed by the Junction of two or more States, or Parts of States, without the Consent of the Legislatures of the States concerned as well as of the Congress.

The Congress shall have Power to dispose of and make all needful Rules and Regulations respecting the Territory or other Property belonging to the United States; and nothing in this Constitution shall be so construed as to Prejudice any Claims of the United States, or of any particular State.

Section 4

The United States shall guarantee to every State in this Union a Republican Form of Government, and shall protect each of them against Invasion; and on Application of the Legislature, or of the Executive (when the Legislature cannot be convened) against domestic Violence.

Article V

The Congress, whenever two thirds of both Houses shall deem it necessary, shall propose Amendments to this Constitution, or, on the Application of the Legislatures of two thirds of the several States, shall call a Convention for proposing Amendments, which, in either Case, shall be valid to all Intents and Purposes, as Part of this Constitution, when ratified by the Legislatures of three fourths of the several States, or by Conventions in three fourths thereof, as the one or the other Mode of Ratification may be proposed by the Congress; Provided that no Amendment which may be made prior to the Year One thousand eight hundred and eight shall in any Manner affect the first and fourth Clauses in the Ninth Section of the first Article; and that no State, without its Consent, shall be deprived of its equal Suffrage in the Senate.

Article VI

All Debts contracted and Engagements entered into, before the Adoption of this Constitution, shall be as valid against the United States under this Constitution, as under the Confederation.

This Constitution, and the Laws of the United States which shall be made in Pursuance thereof; and all Treaties made, or which shall be made, under the Authority of the United States, shall be the supreme Law of the Land; and the Judges in every State shall be bound thereby, any Thing in the Constitution or Laws of any State to the Contrary notwithstanding.

The Senators and Representatives before mentioned, and the Members of the several State Legislatures, and all executive and judicial Officers, both of the United States and of the several States, shall be bound by Oath or Affirmation, to support this Constitution; but no religious Test shall ever be required as a Qualification to any Office or public Trust under the United States.

Article VII

The Ratification of the Conventions of nine States, shall be sufficient for the Establishment of this Constitution between the States so ratifying the Same.

First Amendment

Congress shall make no law respecting an establishment of religion, or prohibiting the free exercise thereof; or abridging the freedom of speech, or of the press; or the right of the people peaceably to assemble, and to petition the Government for a redress of grievances.

Second Amendment

A well regulated Militia, being necessary to the security of a free State, the right of the people to keep and bear Arms, shall not be infringed.

Third Amendment

No Soldier shall, in time of peace be quartered in any house, without the consent of the Owner, nor in time of war, but in a manner to be prescribed by law.

Fourth Amendment

The right of the people to be secure in their persons, houses, papers, and effects, against unreasonable searches and seizures, shall not be violated, and no Warrants shall issue, but upon probable cause, supported by Oath or affirmation, and particularly describing the place to be searched, and the persons or things to be seized.

Fifth Amendment

No person shall be held to answer for a capital, or otherwise infamous crime, unless on a presentment or indictment of a Grand Jury, except in cases arising in the land or naval forces, or in the Militia, when in actual service in time of War or public danger; nor shall any person be subject for the same offence to be twice put in jeopardy of life or limb; nor shall be compelled in any criminal case to be a witness against himself, nor be deprived of life, liberty, or property, without due process of law; nor shall private property be taken for public use, without just compensation.

Sixth Amendment

In all criminal prosecutions, the accused shall enjoy the right to a speedy and public trial, by an impartial jury of the State and district wherein the crime shall have been committed, which district shall have been previously ascertained by law, and to be informed of the nature and cause of the accusation; to be confronted with the witnesses against him; to have compulsory process for obtaining witnesses in his favor, and to have the Assistance of Counsel for his defence.

Seventh Amendment

In Suits at common law, where the value in controversy shall exceed twenty dollars, the right of trial by jury shall be preserved, and no fact tried by a jury, shall be otherwise reexamined in any Court of the United States, than according to the rules of the common law.

Eighth Amendment

Excessive bail shall not be required, nor excessive fines imposed, nor cruel and unusual punishments inflicted.

Ninth Amendment

The enumeration in the Constitution, of certain rights, shall not be construed to deny or disparage others retained by the people.

10th Amendment

The powers not delegated to the United States by the Constitution, nor prohibited by it to the States, are reserved to the States respectively, or to the people.

11th Amendment

The Judicial power of the United States shall not be construed to extend to any suit in law or equity, commenced or prosecuted against one of the United States by Citizens of another State, or by Citizens or Subjects of any Foreign State.

12th Amendment

The Electors shall meet in their respective states and vote by ballot for President and Vice-President, one of whom, at least, shall not be an inhabitant of the same state with themselves; they shall name in their ballots the person voted for as President, and in distinct ballots the person voted for as Vice-President, and they shall make distinct lists of all persons voted for as President, and of all persons voted for as Vice-President, and of the number of votes for each, which lists they shall sign and certify, and transmit sealed to the seat of the government of the United States, directed to the President of the Senate; — The President of the Senate shall, in the presence of the Senate and House of Representatives, open all the certificates and the votes shall then be counted; — The person having the greatest number of votes for President, shall be the President, if such number be a majority of the whole number of Electors appointed; and if no person have such majority, then from the persons having the highest numbers not exceeding three on the list of those voted for as President, the House of Representatives shall choose immediately, by ballot, the President. But in choosing the President, the votes shall be taken by states, the representation from each state having one vote; a quorum for this purpose shall consist of a member or members from two-thirds of the states, and a majority of all the states shall be necessary to a choice. And if the House of Representatives shall not choose a President whenever the right of choice shall devolve upon them, before the fourth day of March next following, then the Vice-President shall act as President, as in case of the death or other constitutional disability of the President.— The person having the greatest number of votes as Vice-President, shall be the Vice-President, if such number be a majority of the whole number of Electors appointed, and if no person have a majority, then from the two highest numbers on the list, the Senate shall choose the Vice-President; a quorum for the purpose shall consist of two-thirds of the whole number of Senators, and a majority of the whole number shall be necessary to a choice. But no person constitutionally ineligible to the office of President shall be eligible to that of Vice-President of the United States.

13th Amendment

Section 1

Neither slavery nor involuntary servitude, except as a punishment for crime whereof the party shall have been duly convicted, shall exist within the United States, or any place subject to their jurisdiction.

Section 2

Congress shall have power to enforce this article by appropriate legislation.

14th Amendment

Section 1

All persons born or naturalized in the United States, and subject to the jurisdiction thereof, are citizens of the United States and of the State wherein they reside. No State shall make or enforce any law which shall abridge the privileges or immunities of citizens of the United States; nor shall any State deprive any person of life, liberty, or property, without due process of law; nor deny to any person within its jurisdiction the equal protection of the laws.

Section 2

Representatives shall be apportioned among the several States according to their respective numbers, counting the whole number of persons in each State, excluding Indians not taxed. But when the right to vote at any election for the choice of electors for President and Vice-President of the United States, Representatives in Congress, the Executive and Judicial officers of a State, or the members of the Legislature thereof, is denied to any of the male inhabitants of such State, being twenty-one years of age, and citizens of the United States, or in any way abridged, except for participation in rebellion, or other crime, the basis of representation therein shall be reduced in the proportion which the number of such male citizens shall bear to the whole number of male citizens twenty-one years of age in such State.

Section 3

No person shall be a Senator or Representative in Congress, or elector of President and Vice-President, or hold any office, civil or military, under the United States, or under any State, who, having previously taken an oath, as a member of Congress, or as an officer of the United States, or as a member of any State legislature, or as an executive or judicial officer of any State, to support the Constitution of the United States, shall have engaged in insurrection or rebellion against the same, or given aid or comfort to the enemies thereof. But Congress may by a vote of two-thirds of each House, remove such disability.

Section 4

The validity of the public debt of the United States, authorized by law, including debts incurred for payment of pensions and bounties for services in suppressing insurrection or rebellion, shall not be questioned. But neither the United States nor any State shall assume or pay any debt or obligation incurred in aid of insurrection or rebellion against the United States, or any claim for the loss or emancipation of any slave; but all such debts, obligations and claims shall be held illegal and void.

Section 5

The Congress shall have the power to enforce, by appropriate legislation, the provisions of this article.

15th Amendment

Section 1

The right of citizens of the United States to vote shall not be denied or abridged by the United States or by any State on account of race, color, or previous condition of servitude.

Section 2

The Congress shall have the power to enforce this article by appropriate legislation.

16th Amendment

The Congress shall have power to lay and collect taxes on incomes, from whatever source derived, without apportionment among the several States, and without regard to any census or enumeration.

17th Amendment

The Senate of the United States shall be composed of two Senators from each State, elected by the people thereof, for six years; and each Senator shall have one vote. The electors in each State shall have the qualifications requisite for electors of the most numerous branch of the State legislatures.

When vacancies happen in the representation of any State in the Senate, the executive authority of such State shall issue writs of election to fill such vacancies: Provided, That the legislature of any State may empower the executive thereof to make temporary appointments until the people fill the vacancies by election as the legislature may direct.

This amendment shall not be so construed as to affect the election or term of any Senator chosen before it becomes valid as part of the Constitution.

18th Amendment

Section 1

After one year from the ratification of this article the manufacture, sale, or transportation of intoxicating liquors within, the importation thereof into, or the exportation thereof from the United States and all territory subject to the jurisdiction thereof for beverage purposes is hereby prohibited.

Section 2

The Congress and the several States shall have concurrent power to enforce this article by appropriate legislation.

Section 3

This article shall be inoperative unless it shall have been ratified as an amendment to the Constitution by the legislatures of the several States, as provided in the Constitution, within seven years from the date of the submission hereof to the States by the Congress.

19th Amendment

The right of citizens of the United States to vote shall not be denied or abridged by the United States or by any State on account of sex.

Congress shall have power to enforce this article by appropriate legislation.

20th Amendment

Section 1

The terms of the President and the Vice President shall end at noon on the 20th day of January, and the terms of Senators and Representatives at noon on the 3d day of January, of the years in which such terms would have ended if this article had not been ratified; and the terms of their successors shall then begin.

Section 2

The Congress shall assemble at least once in every year, and such meeting shall begin at noon on the 3d day of January, unless they shall by law appoint a different day.

Section 3

If, at the time fixed for the beginning of the term of the President, the President elect shall have died, the Vice President elect shall become President. If a President shall not have been chosen before the time fixed for the beginning of his term, or if the President elect shall have failed to qualify, then the Vice President elect shall act as President until a President shall have qualified; and the Congress may by law provide for the case wherein neither a President elect nor a Vice President shall have qualified, declaring who shall then act as President, or the manner in which one who is to act shall be selected, and such person shall act accordingly until a President or Vice President shall have qualified.

Section 4

The Congress may by law provide for the case of the death of any of the persons from whom the House of Representatives may choose a President whenever the right of choice shall have devolved upon them, and for the case of the death of any of the persons from whom the Senate may choose a Vice President whenever the right of choice shall have devolved upon them.

Section 5

Sections 1 and 2 shall take effect on the 15th day of October following the ratification of this article.

Section 6

This article shall be inoperative unless it shall have been ratified as an amendment to the Constitution by the legislatures of three-fourths of the several States within seven years from the date of its submission.

21st Amendment

Section 1

The eighteenth article of amendment to the Constitution of the United States is hereby repealed.

Section 2

The transportation or importation into any State, Territory, or Possession of the United States for delivery or use therein of intoxicating liquors, in violation of the laws thereof, is hereby prohibited.

Section 3

This article shall be inoperative unless it shall have been ratified as an amendment to the Constitution by conventions in the several States, as provided in the Constitution, within seven years from the date of the submission hereof to the States by the Congress.

22nd Amendment

Section 1

No person shall be elected to the office of the President more than twice, and no person who has held the office of President, or acted as President, for more than two years of a term to which some other person was elected President shall be elected to the office of

President more than once. But this Article shall not apply to any person holding the office of President when this Article was proposed by Congress, and shall not prevent any person who may be holding the office of President, or acting as President, during the term within which this Article becomes operative from holding the office of President or acting as President during the remainder of such term.

Section 2

This article shall be inoperative unless it shall have been ratified as an amendment to the Constitution by the legislatures of three-fourths of the several States within seven years from the date of its submission to the States by the Congress.

23rd Amendment

Section 1

The District constituting the seat of Government of the United States shall appoint in such manner as Congress may direct:

A number of electors of President and Vice President equal to the whole number of Senators and Representatives in Congress to which the District would be entitled if it were a State, but in no event more than the least populous State; they shall be in addition to those appointed by the States, but they shall be considered, for the purposes of the election of President and Vice President, to be electors appointed by a State; and they shall meet in the District and perform such duties as provided by the twelfth article of amendment.

Section 2

The Congress shall have power to enforce this article by appropriate legislation.

24th Amendment

Section 1

The right of citizens of the United States to vote in any primary or other election for President or Vice President, for electors for President or Vice President, or for Senator or Representative in Congress, shall not be denied or abridged by the United States or any State by reason of failure to pay poll tax or other tax.

Section 2

The Congress shall have power to enforce this article by appropriate legislation.

25th Amendment

Section 1

In case of the removal of the President from office or of his death or resignation, the Vice President shall become President.

Section 2

Whenever there is a vacancy in the office of the Vice President, the President shall nominate a Vice President who shall take office upon confirmation by a majority vote of both Houses of Congress.

Section 3

Whenever the President transmits to the President pro tempore of the Senate and the Speaker of the House of Representatives his written declaration that he is unable to discharge the powers and duties of his office, and until he transmits to them a written declaration to the contrary, such powers and duties shall be discharged by the Vice President as Acting President.

Section 4

Whenever the Vice President and a majority of either the principal officers of the executive departments or of such other body as Congress may by law provide, transmit to the President pro tempore of the Senate and the Speaker of the House of Representatives their written declaration that the President is unable to discharge the powers and duties of his office, the Vice President shall immediately assume the powers and duties of the office as Acting President.

Thereafter, when the President transmits to the President pro tempore of the Senate and the Speaker of the House of Representatives his written declaration that no inability exists, he shall resume the powers and duties of his office unless the Vice President and a majority of either the principal officers of the executive department or of such other body as Congress may by law provide, transmit within four days to the President pro tempore of the Senate and the Speaker of the House of Representatives their written declaration that the President is unable to discharge the powers and duties of his office. Thereupon Congress shall decide the issue, assembling within forty-eight hours for that purpose if not in session. If the Congress, within twenty-one days after receipt of the latter written declaration, or, if Congress is not in session, within twenty-one days after Congress is required to assemble, determines by two-thirds vote of both Houses that the President is unable to discharge the powers and duties of his office, the Vice President shall continue to discharge the same as Acting President; otherwise, the President shall resume the powers and duties of his office.

26th Amendment

Section 1

The right of citizens of the United States, who are eighteen years of age or older, to vote shall not be denied or abridged by the United States or by any State on account of age.

Section 2

The Congress shall have power to enforce this article by appropriate legislation.

27th Amendment

No law, varying the compensation for the services of the Senators and Representatives, shall take effect, until an election of representatives shall have intervened.

Appendix D

"The Constitution of the United States: Is It
Pro-Slavery or Anti-Slavery?"

Frederick Douglass, 1860

I proceed to the discussion. And first a word about the question. Much will be gained at the outset if we fully and clearly understand the real question under discussion. Indeed, nothing is or can be understood. This are often confounded and treated as the same, for no better reason than that they resemble each other, even while they are in their nature and character totally distinct and even directly opposed to each other. This jumbling up things is a sort of dust-throwing which is often indulged in by small men who argue for victory rather than for truth.

Thus, for instance, the American Government and the American Constitution are spoken of in a manner which would naturally lead the hearer to believe that one is identical with the other; when the truth is, they are distinct in character as is a ship and a compass. The one may point right and the other steer wrong. A chart is one thing, the course of the vessel is another. The Constitution may be right, the Government is wrong. If the Government has been governed by mean, sordid, and wicked passions, it does not follow that the Constitution is mean, sordid, and wicked.

What, then, is the question? I will state it. But first let me state what is not the question. It is not whether slavery existed in the United States at the time of the adoption of the Constitution; it is not whether slaveholders took part in the framing of the Constitution; it is not whether those slaveholders, in their hearts, intended to secure certain advantages in that instrument for slavery; it is not whether the American Government has been wielded during seventy-two years in favour of the propagation and permanence of slavery; it is not whether a pro-slavery interpretation has been put upon the Constitution by the American Courts—all these points may be true or they may be false, they may be accepted or they may be rejected, without in any wise affecting the real question in debate.

The real and exact question between myself and the class of persons represented by the speech at the City Hall may be fairly stated thus:—1st, Does the United States Constitution guarantee to any class or description of people in that country the right to enslave, or hold as property, any other class or description of people in that country? 2nd, Is the dissolution of the union between the slave and free States required by fidelity to the slaves, or by the just demands of conscience? Or, in other words, is the refusal to exercise the elective franchise, and to hold office in America, the surest, wisest, and best way to abolish slavery in America?

To these questions the Garrisonians say Yes. They hold the Constitution to be a slaveholding instrument, and will not cast a vote or hold office, and denounce all who vote or hold office, no matter how faithfully such persons labour to promote the abolition of slavery. I, on the other hand, deny that the Constitution guarantees the right to hold property in man, and believe that the way to abolish slavery in America is to vote such men into power as well use their powers for the abolition of slavery. This is the issue plainly stated, and you shall judge between us. Before we examine into the disposition, tendency, and character of the Constitution, I think we had better ascertain what the Constitution itself is. Before looking for what it means, let us see what it is. Here, too, there is much dust to be cleared away. What, then, is the Constitution? I will tell you. It is not even like the British Constitution, which is made up of enactments of Parliament, decisions of Courts, and the established usages of the Government. The American Constitution is a written instrument full and complete in itself. No Court in America, no Congress, no President, can add a single word thereto, or take a single word thereto. It is a great national enactment done by the people, and can only be altered, amended, or added to by the people. I am careful to make this statement here; in America it would not be necessary. It would not be necessary here if my assailant had shown the same desire to be set before you the simple truth, which he manifested to make out a good case for himself and friends. Again, it should be borne in mind that the mere text, and only the text, and not any commentaries or creeds written by those who wished to give the text a meaning apart from its plain reading, was adopted as the Constitution of the United States. It should also be borne in mind that the intentions of those who framed the Constitution, be they good or bad, for slavery or against slavery, are so respected so far, and so far only, as we find those intentions plainly stated in the Constitution. It would be the wildest of absurdities, and lead to endless confusion and mischiefs, if, instead of looking to the written paper itself, for its meaning, it were attempted to make us search it out, in the secret motives, and dishonest intentions, of some of the men who took part in writing it. It was what they said that was adopted by the people, not what they were ashamed or afraid to say, and really omitted to say. Bear in mind, also, and the fact is an important one, that the framers of the Constitution sat with doors closed, and that this was done purposely, that nothing but the result of their labours should be seen, and that that result should be judged of by the people free from any of the bias shown in the debates. It should also be borne in mind, and the fact is still more important, that the debates in the convention that framed the Constitution, and by means of which a pro-slavery interpretation is now attempted to be forced upon that instrument, were not published till more than a quarter of a century after the presentation and the adoption of the Constitution.

These debates were purposely kept out of view, in order that the people should adopt, not the secret motives or unexpressed intentions of any body, but the simple text of the paper itself. Those debates form no part of the original agreement. I repeat, the paper itself, and only the paper itself, with its own plainly written purposes, is the Constitution. It must stand or fall, flourish or fade, on its own individual and self-declared character and objects. Again, where would be the advantage of a written Constitution, if, instead of seeking its meaning in its words, we had to seek them in the secret intentions of individuals who may have had something to do with writing the paper? What will the people of America a hundred years hence care about the intentions of the scriveners who wrote the Constitution? These men are already gone from us, and in the course of nature were expected to go from us. They were for a generation, but the Constitution is for ages. Whatever we may owe to them, we certainly owe it to ourselves, and to mankind, and to God, to maintain the truth of our own language, and to allow no villainy, not even the villainy of holding men as slaves—which Wesley says is the sum of all villainies—to shelter itself under a fair-seeming and virtuous language. We owe it to ourselves to compel the devil to wear his own garments, and to make wicked laws speak out their wicked intentions. Common sense, and common justice, and sound rules of interpretation all drive us to the words of the law for the meaning of the law. The practice of the Government is dwelt upon with much fervour and eloquence as conclusive as to the slaveholding character of the Constitution. This is really the strong point and the only strong point, made in the speech in the City Hall. But good as this argument is, it is not conclusive. A wise man has said that few people have been found better than their laws, but many have been found worse. To this last rule America is no exception. Her laws are one thing, her practice is another thing. We read that the Jews made void the law by their tradition, that Moses permitted men to put away their wives because of the hardness of their hearts, but that this was not so at the beginning. While good laws will always be found where good practice prevails, the reverse does not always hold true. Far from it. The very opposite is often the case. What then? Shall we condemn the righteous law because wicked men twist it to the support of wickedness? Is that the way to deal with good and evil? Shall we blot out all distinction between them, and hand over to slavery all that slavery may claim on the score of long practice? Such is the course commended to us in the City Hall speech. After all, the fact that men go out of the Constitution to prove it pro-slavery, whether that going out is to the practice of the Government, or to the secret intentions of the writers of the paper, the fact that they do go out is very significant. It is a powerful argument on my side. It is an admission that the thing for which they are looking is not to be found where only it ought to be found, and that is in the Constitution itself. If it is not there, it is nothing to the purpose, be it wheresoever else it may be. But I shall have no more to say on this point hereafter.

The very eloquent lecturer at the City Hall doubtless felt some embarrassment from the fact that he had literally to give the Constitution a pro-slavery interpretation; because upon its face it of itself conveys no such meaning, but a very opposite meaning. He thus sums up what he calls the slaveholding provisions of the Constitution. I quote his own words:—"Article 1, section 9, provides for the continuance of the African slave trade for the 20 years, after the adoption of the Constitution. Art. 4, section 9, provides for the recovery from the other States of fugitive slaves. Art. 1, section 2, gives the slave States a representation of the three-fifths of all the slave population; and Art. 1, section 8, requires the President to use the military, naval, ordnance, and militia resources of the entire country for the suppression of slave insurrection, in the same manner as he would employ them to repel invasion." Now any man reading this statement, or hearing it made with such a show of exactness, would unquestionably suppose that he speaker or writer had given the plain written text of the Constitution itself. I can hardly believe that the intended to make any such impression. It would be a scandalous imputation to say he did. Any yet what are we to make of it? How can we regard it? How can he be screened from the charge of having perpetrated a deliberate and point-blank misrepresentation? That individual has seen fit to place himself before the public as my opponent, and yet I would gladly find some excuse for him. I do not wish to think as badly of him as this trick of his would naturally lead me to think. Why did he not read the Constitution? Why did he read that which was not the Constitution? He pretended to be giving chapter and verse, section and clause, paragraph and provision. The words of the Constitution were before him. Why then did he not give you the plain words of the Constitution? Oh, sir, I fear that the gentleman knows too well why he did not. It so happens that no such words as "African slave trade," no such words as "slave insurrections," are anywhere used in that instrument. These are the words of that orator, and not the words of the Constitution of the United States. Now you shall see a slight difference between my manner of treating this subject and what which my opponent has seen fit, for reasons satisfactory to himself, to pursue. What he withheld, that I will spread before you: what he suppressed, I will bring to light: and what he passed over in silence, I will proclaim: that you may have the whole case before you, and not be left to depend upon either his, or upon my inferences or testimony. Here then are several provisions of the Constitution to which reference has been made. I read them word for word just as they stand in the paper, called the United States Constitution, Art. I, sec. 2. "Representatives and direct taxes shall be apportioned among the several States which may be included in this Union, according to their respective numbers, which shall be determined by adding to the whole number of free persons, including those bound to service for a term years, and excluding Indians not taxed, three-fifths of all other persons; Art. I, sec. 9. The migration or importation of such persons as any of the States now existing shall think fit to admit, shall not be prohibited by the Congress prior to the year one thousand eight hundred and eight, but a tax or duty may be imposed on such importation, not exceeding tend dollars for each person; Art. 4, sec. 2. No person held to service or labour in one State, under the laws thereof, escaping into another shall, in consequence of any law or regulation therein, be discharged from service or labour; but shall be delivered up on claim of the party to whom such service or labour may be due; Art. I, sec. 8. To provide for calling for the militia to execute the laws of the Union, suppress insurrections, and repel invasions." Here then, are those provisions of the Constitution, which the most extravagant defenders of slavery can claim to guarantee a right of property in man. These are the provisions which have been pressed into the service of the human fleshmongers of America. Let us look at them just as they stand, one by one. Let us grant, for the sake of the argument, that the first of these provisions, referring to the basis of representation and taxation, does refer to slaves. We are not compelled to make that admission, for it might fairly apply to aliens—persons living in the country, but not naturalized. But giving the provisions the very worse construction, what does it amount to? I answer—It is a downright disability laid upon the slaveholding States; one which deprives those States of two-fifths of their natural basis of representation. A black man in a free State is worth just two-fifths more than a black man in a slave State, as a basis of political power under the Constitution. Therefore, instead of encouraging slavery, the Constitution encourages freedom by giving an increase of "two-fifths" of political power to free over slave States. So much for the three-fifths clause; taking it at is worst, it still leans to freedom, not slavery; for, be it remembered that the Constitution nowhere forbids a coloured man to vote. I come to the next, that which it is said guaranteed the continuance of the African slave trade for twenty years. I will also take that for just what my opponent alleges it to have been, although the Constitution does not warrant any such conclusion. But, to be liberal, let us suppose it did, and what follows? Why, this—that this part of the Constitution, so far as the slave trade is concerned, became a dead letter more than 50 years ago, and now binds no man's conscience for the continuance of any slave trade whatsoever. Mr. Thompson is just 52 years too late in dissolving the Union on account of this clause. He might as well dissolve the British Government, because Queen Elizabeth granted to Sir John Hawkins to import Africans into the West Indies 300 years ago! But there is still more to be said about this abolition of the slave trade. Men, at that time, both in England and in America, looked upon the slave trade as the life of slavery. The abolition of the slave trade was supposed to be the certain death of slavery. Cut off the stream, and the pond will dry up, was the common notion at the time.

Wilberforce and Clarkson, clear-sighted as they were, took this view; and the American statesmen, in providing for the abolition of the slave trade, thought they were providing for the abolition of the slavery. This view is quite consistent with the history of the times. All regarded slavery as an expiring and doomed system, destined to speedily disappear from the country. But, again, it should be remembered that this very provision, if made to refer to the African slave trade at all, makes the Constitution anti-slavery rather than for slavery; for it says to the slave States, the price you will have to pay for coming into the American Union is, that the slave trade, which you would carry on indefinitely out of the Union, shall be put an end to in twenty years if you come into the Union. Secondly, if it does apply, it expired by its own limitation more than fifty years ago. Thirdly, it is anti-slavery, because it looked to the abolition of slavery rather than to its perpetuity. Fourthly, it showed that the intentions of the framers of the Constitution were good, not bad. I think this is quite enough for this point.

I go to the "slave insurrection" clause, though, in truth, there is no such clause. The one which is called so has nothing whatever to do with slaves or slaveholders any more than your laws for suppression of popular outbreaks has to do with making slaves of you and your children. It is only a law for suppression of riots or insurrections. But I will be generous here, as well as elsewhere, and grant that it applies to slave insurrections. Let us suppose that an anti-slavery man is President of the United States (and the day that shall see this the case is not distant) and this very power of suppressing slave insurrections would put an end to slavery. The right to put down an insurrection carries with it the right to determine the means by which it shall be put down. If it should turn out that slavery is a source of insurrection, that there is no security from insurrection while slavery lasts, why, the Constitution would be best obeyed by putting an end to slavery, and an anti-slavery Congress would do the very same thing. Thus, you see, the so-called slave-holding provisions of the American Constitution, which a little while ago looked so formidable, are, after all, no defence or guarantee for slavery whatever. But there is one other provision. This is called the "Fugitive Slave Provision." It is called so by those who wish to make it subserve the interest of slavery in America, and the same by those who wish to uphold the views of a party in this country. It is put thus in the speech at the City Hall:—"Let us go back to 1787, and enter Liberty Hall, Philadelphia, where sat in convention the illustrious men who framed the Constitution—with George Washington in the chair. On the 27th of September, Mr. Butler and Mr. Pinckney, two delegates from the State of South Carolina, moved that the Constitution should require that fugitive slaves and servants should be delivered up like criminals, and after a discussion on the subject, the clause, as it stands in the Constitution, was adopted. After this, in the conventions held in the several States to ratify the Constitution, the same meaning was attached to the words. For example, Mr. Madison (afterwards President), when recommending the Constitution to his constituents, told them that the clause would secure them their property in slaves." I must ask you to look well to this statement. Upon its face, it would seem a full and fair statement of the history of the transaction it professes to describe and yet I declare unto you, knowing as I do the facts in the case, my utter amazement at the downright untruth conveyed under the fair seeming words now quoted. The man who could make such a statement may have all the craftiness of a lawyer, but who can accord to him the candour of an honest debater? What could more completely destroy all confidence in his statements? Mark you, the orator had not allowed his audience to hear read the provision of the Constitution to which he referred. He merely characterized it as one to "deliver up fugitive slaves and servants like criminals," and tells you that this was done "after discussion." But he took good care not to tell you what was the nature of that discussion. He have would have spoiled the whole effect of his statement had he told you the whole truth. Now, what are the facts connected with this provision of the Constitution? You shall have them. It seems to take two men to tell the truth. It is quite true that Mr. Butler and Mr. Pinckney introduced a provision expressly with a view to the recapture of fugitive slaves: it is quite true also that there was some discussion on the subject—and just here the truth shall come out. These illustrious kidnappers were told promptly in that discussion that no such idea as property in man should be admitted into the Constitution. The speaker in question might have told you, and he would have told you but the simple truth, if he had told you that he proposition of Mr. Butler and Mr. Pinckney—which he leads you to infer was adopted by the convention that from the Constitution—was, in fact, promptly and indignantly rejected by that convention. He might have told you, had it suited his purpose to do so, that the words employed in the first draft of the fugitive slave clause were such as applied to the condition of slaves, and expressly declared that persons held to "servitude" should be given up; but that the word "servitude" was struck from the provision, for the very reason that it applied to slaves. He might have told you that the same Mr. Madison declared that the word was struck out because the convention would not consent that the idea of property in men should be admitted into the Constitution. The fact that Mr. Madison can be cited on both sides of this question is another evidence of the folly and absurdity of making the secret intentions of the framers the criterion by which the Constitution is to be construed. But it may be asked—if this clause does not apply to slaves, to whom does it apply?

I answer, that when adopted, it applies to a very large class of persons—namely, redemptioners—persons who had come to America from Holland, from Ireland, and other quarters of the globe—like the Coolies to the West Indies—and had, for a consideration duly paid, become bound to "serve and labour" for the parties two whom their service and labour was due. It applies to indentured apprentices and others who have become bound for a consideration, under contract duly made, to serve and labour, to such persons this provision applies, and only to such persons. The plain reading of this provision shows that it applies, and that it can only properly and legally apply, to persons "bound to service." Its object plainly is, to secure the fulfillment of contracts for "service and labour." It applies to indentured apprentices, and any other persons from whom service and labour may be due. The legal condition of the slave puts him beyond the operation of this provision. He is not described in it. He is a simple article of property. He does not owe and cannot owe service. He cannot even make a contract. It is impossible for him to do so. He can no more make such a contract than a horse or an ox can make one. This provision, then, only respects persons who owe service, and they only can owe service who can receive an equivalent and make a bargain. The slave cannot do that, and is therefore exempted from the operation of this fugitive provision. In all matters where laws are taught to be made the means of oppression, cruelty, and wickedness, I am for strict construction. I will concede nothing. It must be shown that it is so nominated in the bond. The pound of flesh, but not one drop of blood. The very nature of law is opposed to all such wickedness, and makes it difficult to accomplish such objects under the forms of law. Law is not merely an arbitrary enactment with regard to justice, reason, or humanity. Blackstone defines

it to be a rule prescribed by the supreme power of the State commanding what is right and forbidding what is wrong. The speaker at
the City Hall laid down some rules of legal interpretation. These rules
send us to the history of the law for its meaning. I have no objection
to such a course in ordinary cases of doubt. But where human liberty
and justice are at stake, the case falls under an entirely different class
of rules. There must be something more than history—something
more than tradition. The Supreme Court of the United States lays
down this rule, and it meets the case exactly—"Where rights are
infringed—where the fundamental principles of the law are
overthrown—where the general system of the law is departed from,
the legislative intention must be expressed with irresistible clearness."
The same court says that the language of the law must be construed
strictly in favour of justice and liberty. Again, there is another rule
of law. It is—Where a law is susceptible of two meanings, the one
making it accomplish an innocent purpose, and the other making it
accomplish a wicked purpose, we must in all cases adopt that which
makes it accomplish an innocent purpose. Again, the details of a law
are to be interpreted in the light of the declared objects sought by the
law. I set these rules down against those employed at the City Hall.
To me they seem just and rational. I only ask you to look at the
American Constitution in the light of them, and you will see with
me that no man is guaranteed a right of property in man, under the
provisions of that instrument. If there are two ideas more distinct in
their character and essence than another, those ideas are "persons"
and "property," "men" and "things." Now, when it is proposed to
transform persons into "property" and men into beasts of burden, I
demand that the law that completes such a purpose shall be expressed
with irresistible clearness. The thing must not be left to inference, but
must be done in plain English. I know how this view of the subject
is treated by the class represented at the City Hall. They are in the

habit of treating the Negro as an exception to general rules. When their own liberty is in question they will avail themselves of all rules of law which protect and defend their freedom; but when the black man's rights are in question they concede everything, admit everything for slavery, and put liberty to the proof. They reserve the common law usage, and presume the Negro a slave unless he can prove himself free. I, on the other hand, presume him free unless he is proved to be otherwise. Let us look at the objects for which the Constitution was framed and adopted, and see if slavery is one of them. Here are its own objects as set forth by itself:—"We, the people of these United States, in order to form a more perfect union, establish justice, ensure domestic tranquility, provide for the common defense, promote the general welfare, and secure the blessings of liberty to ourselves and our posterity, do ordain and establish this Constitution of the United States of America." The objects here set forth are six in number: union, defence, welfare, tranquility, justice, and liberty. These are all good objects, and slavery, so far from being among them, is a foe of them all. But it has been said that Negroes are not included within the benefits sought under this declaration. This is said by the slaveholders in America—it is said by the City Hall orator—but it is not said by the Constitution itself. Its language is "we the people;" not we the white people, not even we the citizens, not we the privileged class, not we the high, not we the low, but we the people; not we the horses, sheep, and swine, and wheel-barrows, but we the people, we the human inhabitants; and, if Negroes are people, they are included in the benefits for which the Constitution of America was ordained and established. But how dare any man who pretends to be a friend to the Negro thus gratuitously concede away what the Negro has a right to claim under the Constitution? Why should such friends invent new arguments to increase the hopelessness of his bondage? This, I undertake to say, as the conclusion of the whole matter, that the constitutionality of slavery can be made out only by disregarding the plain and common-sense reading of the Constitution itself; by discrediting and casting away as worthless the most beneficent rules of legal interpretation; by ruling the Negro outside of these beneficent rules; by claiming that the Constitution does not mean what it says, and that it says what it does not mean; by disregarding the written Constitution, and interpreting it in the light of a secret understanding. It is in this mean, contemptible, and underhand method that the American Constitution is pressed into the service of slavery. They go everywhere else for proof that the Constitution declares that no person shall be deprived of life, liberty, or property without due process of law; it secures to every man the right of trial by jury, the privilege of the writ of habeas corpus—the great writ that put an end to slavery and slave-hunting in England—and it secures to every State a republican form of government. Anyone of these provisions in the hands of abolition statesmen, and backed up by a right moral sentiment, would put an end to slavery in America. The Constitution forbids the passing of a bill of attainder: that is, a law entailing upon the child the disabilities and hardships imposed upon the parent. Every slave law in America might be repealed on this very ground. The slave is made a slave because his mother is a slave. But to all this it is said that the practice of the American people is against my view. I admit it. They have given the Constitution a slaveholding interpretation. I admit it. Thy have committed innumerable wrongs against the Negro in the name of the Constitution. Yes, I admit it all; and I go with him who goes farthest in denouncing these wrongs. But it does not follow that the Constitution is in favour of these wrongs because the slaveholders have given it that interpretation. To be consistent in his logic, the City Hall speaker must follow the example of some of his brothers in America—he must not only fling away the Constitution, but the

Bible. The Bible must follow the Constitution, for that, too, has been interpreted for slavery by American divines. Nay, more, he must not stop with the Constitution of America, but make war with the British Constitution, for, if I mistake not, the gentleman is opposed to the union of Church and State. In America he called himself a Republican. Yet he does not go for breaking down the British Constitution, although you have a Queen on the throne, and bishops in the House of Lords.

My argument against the dissolution of the American Union is this: It would place the slave system more exclusively under the control of the slaveholding States, and withdraw it from the power in the Northern States which is opposed to slavery. Slavery is essentially barbarous in its character. It, above all things else, dreads the presence of an advanced civilization. It flourishes best where it meets no reproving frowns, and hears no condemning voices. While in the Union it will meet with both. Its hope of life, in the last resort, is to get out of the Union. I am, therefore, for drawing the bond of the Union more completely under the power of the Free States. What they most dread, that I most desire. I have much confidence in the instincts of the slaveholders. They see that the Constitution will afford slavery no protection when it shall cease to be administered by slaveholders. They see, moreover, that if there is once a will in the people of America to abolish slavery, this is no word, no syllable in the Constitution to forbid that result. They see that the Constitution has not saved slavery in Rhode Island, in Connecticut, in New York, or Pennsylvania; that the Free States have only added three to their original number. There were twelve Slave States at the beginning of the Government: there are fifteen now. They dissolution of the Union would not give the North a single advantage over slavery, but would take from it many. Within the Union we have a firm basis of opposition to slavery. It is opposed to all the great objects of the Constitution.

The dissolution of the Union is not only an unwise but a cowardly measure—15 millions running away from three hundred and fifty thousand slaveholders. Mr. Garrison and his friends tell us that while in the Union we are responsible for slavery. He and they sing out "No Union with slaveholders," and refuse to vote. I admit our responsibility for slavery while in the Union but I deny that going out of the Union would free us from that responsibility. There now clearly is no freedom from responsibility for slavery to any American citizen short to the abolition of slavery. The American people have gone quite too far in this slaveholding business now to sum up their whole business of slavery by singing out the cant phrase, "No union with slaveholders." To desert the family hearth may place the recreant husband out of the presence of his starving children, but this does not free him from responsibility. If a man were on board of a pirate ship, and in company with others had robbed and plundered, his whole duty would not be preformed simply by taking the longboat and singing out, "No union with pirates." His duty would be to restore the stolen property. The American people in the Northern States have helped to enslave the black people. Their duty will not have been done till they give them back their plundered rights. Reference was made at the City Hall to my having once held other opinions, and very different opinions to those I have now expressed. An old speech of mine delivered fourteen years ago was read to show—I know not what. Perhaps it was to show that I am not infallible. If so, I have to say in defence, that I never pretended to be. Although I cannot accuse myself of being remarkably unstable, I do not pretend that I have never altered my opinion both in respect to men and things. Indeed, I have been very much modified both in feeling and opinion within the last fourteen years. When I escaped from slavery, and was introduced to the Garrisonians, I adopted very many of their opinions, and defended them just as long as I deemed them true. I was young, had read but little, and naturally took some things on trust. Subsequent experience and reading have led me to examine for myself. This had brought me to other conclusions. When I was a child, I thought and spoke as a child. But the question is not as to what were my opinions fourteen years ago, but what they are now. If I am right now, it really does not matter what I was fourteen years ago. My position now is one of reform, not of revolution. I would act for the abolition of slavery through the Government—not over its ruins. If slaveholders have ruled the American Government for the last fifty years, let the anti-slavery men rule the nation for the next fifty years. If the South has made the Constitution bend to the purposes of slavery, let the North now make that instrument bend to the cause of freedom and justice. If 350,000 slaveholders have, by devoting their energies to that single end, been able to make slavery the vital and animating spirit of the American Confederacy for the last 72 years, now let the freemen of the North, who have the power in their own hands, and who can make the American Government just what they think fit, resolve to blot out for ever the foul and haggard crime, which is the blight and mildew, the curse and the disgrace of the whole United States.

NOTES

Preface

1. The facts explained and opinions expressed in this book are based solely on my own upbringing, experiences, and observations.

Chapter 1: Introduction

1. This introduction is adapted from a slightly shorter article I wrote for *National Review*: Andre Archie, "Color-Blindness Should Be the Norm," *National Review*, July 9, 2020, https://www.nationalreview.com/magazine/2020/07/27/color -blindness-should-be-the-norm.

2. Evan P. Apfelbaum, Michael I. Norton, and Samuel R. Sommers, "Racial Colorblindness: Emergence, Practice, and Implications," *Current Directions in Psychological Science* 21, no. 3 (June 2012): 205–9, https://doi. org/10.1177/0963721411434980.

3. Parents Involved in Community Schools v. Seattle School Dist. No. 1, 551 U.S. 701 (2007).

4. John Stuart Mill, *On Liberty* (New York: Macmillan Publishing, 1956), 21.

5. It must not be forgotten that Mill's liberty principle doesn't apply to humans *qua* humans, it only applies to the civilized, educated elite: "Despotism is a legitimate mode of government in dealing with barbarians, provided the end be their improvement, and the means justified by actually effecting that end. Liberty, as a principle, has no application to any state of things anterior to the time when mankind have become capable of being improved by free and equal discussion. Until then, there is nothing for them but implicit obedience

to an Akbar or a Charlemagne, if they are so fortunate as to find one." Ibid., 14. Cf. Mill's plural voting scheme in his *Thoughts on Parliamentary Reform*.

6. Plessy v. Ferguson, 163 U.S. 537 (1896).
7. Kate Taylor, "Accusations and Rancor as Elite School's Leader Departs," *New York Times*, July 12, 2017, https://www.nytimes.com/2017/07/12/nyregion/ethical-culture-fieldston-school-principal.html.
8. Lyndon B. Johnson, "To Fulfill These Rights," commencement address at Howard University delivered on June 4, 1965, https://www.presidency.ucsb .edu/documents/commencement-address-howard-university-fulfill-these -rights.
9. Regents of the University of California v. Bakke, 438 U.S. 265 (1978).

Chapter 2: Potatoes

1. Ralph Ellison, "The Little Man at Chehaw Station" in *The Collected Essays of Ralph Ellison*, John F. Callahan, ed. (New York: Modern Library 1995), 493.
2. See Books I–VI of Volume II, Aristotle, *The Complete Works of Aristotle*, J. Barnes, ed. (Princeton, New Jersey: Princeton University Press, 1984).
3. Ken Hamblin, *Pick a Better Country* (New York: Simon & Schuster, 1996).
4. W. E. B. Du Bois, *The Souls of Black Folk* in *The Norton Anthology of African American Literature* (New York: W. W. Norton & Company 1997), 665.
5. Ellison, "The World and the Jug" in *The Collected Essays of Ralph Ellison*, 1555.
6. Frank Snowden, "Bernal's 'Blacks' and the Afrocentrists" in *Black Athena Revisited*, Mary R. Lefkowitz and Guy MacLean Rogers, eds. (Chapel Hill: The University of North Carolina Press 1996), 123.

Chapter 3: What Is the Color-Blind Approach to Race Relations?

1. Martin Luther King Jr., "I Have a Dream," transcript of speech delivered during the March on Washington for Jobs and Freedom on August 28, 1963, https://www.archives.gov/files/social-media/transcripts/transcript-march-pt3-of -3-2602934.pdf.
2. Martin Luther King Jr., "Letter from a Birmingham Jail" in *The Norton Anthology of African American Literature* (New York: W. W. Norton & Company, 1997), 1866.
3. I'm specifically referring to generational African Americans, those black Americans that descend from slaves that resided in the contiguous United States prior to the Civil War of 1861.

4. There are several versions of *eudaemonism*. See G. Vlastos's "Happiness and Virtue in Socrates' Moral Theory" in *Socrates: Ironist, Moral Philosopher* (Ithaca: Cornell University Press, 1991), 200–32. The version spoken of here is that of Socrates, Plato, and Aristotle's version.

5. John Stuart Mill, *Utilitarianism* (London: Parker, Son, and Bourn, 1863).

6. These types of plans are based on the self-proclaimed Marxist and political scientist John Roemer's EOp (Equal Opportunity) function. The EOp function informs public policy as a social intervention tool (i.e., affirmative action) designed to promote equal opportunity among groups and individuals.

7. The ancient Greek term for such choices is called *prohairesis*.

8. Plato, *Apology*, trans. G. M. A. Grube (Indianapolis: Hackett Publishing Company, 1992), 29e–30b.

9. Socrates is mentioned by name several times in King's "Letter from a Birmingham Jail."

10. Jonathan Barnes, *The Complete Works of Aristotle*, vol. II (Princeton, New Jersey: Princeton University Press, 1984), 1114a3–13.

11. *Cicero: De Senectute, De Amicitia, De Divinatione*, trans. William Armistead Falconer (Cambridge, Massachusetts: Harvard University Press, 1923), 49–50.

12. Asia, Africa, and South America in particular have experienced these types of movements.

13. Frederick Douglass, *My Bondage and My Freedom* (Chicago: University of Illinois Press, 1987), 100–1.

14. Caleb Bingham, ed., "Dialogue between a Master and Slave," *The Columbian Orator* (Boston: Manning & Loring, 1797), 240; see Appendix for full dialogue.

Chapter 4: Frederick Douglass and the Abolitionists: The Anti-Slavery, Color-Blind Constitution

1. Frederick Douglass, *My Bondage and My Freedom* (Chicago: University of Illinois Press, 1987), 216.

2. "Remarks at Faneuil Hall Meeting on October 30, 1842," *The Liberator*, November 11, 1842.

3. William M. Wiecek, *The Sources of Antislavery Constitutionalism in America 1760–1848* (London: Cornell University Press, 1977), 238

4. Ibid., 238. Also see Evan Lewis, *An Address to Christians of All Denominations on the Inconsistency of Admitting Slave-Holders to Communion and Church Membership* (Philadelphia: S. C. Atkins, 1831).

5. Wiecek, *The Sources of Antislavery Constitutionalism in America 1760–1848*, 238.
6. "Prospectus of the *Liberator* Volume VIII," *The Liberator*, December 15, 1837.
7. Wiecek, 232.
8. Wendell Phillips, *Review of Lysander Spooner's Essay on the Unconstitutionality of Slavery* (Boston: Andrews and Prentis, 1847), 7.
9. Ibid., 15.
10. Wiecek, 242.
11. See Ibid., 116, on the "trustee theory" of congressional power.
12. See *The Founders' Constitution*: Volume 4, Article 4, Section 2, Clause 3, Document 2, University of Chicago Press, 1771, http://press-pubs.uchicago.edu/founders/documents/a4_2_3s2.html.
13. Wiecek, 244.
14. Ibid., 244–45.
15. Disunion, *Address of the American Anti-Slavery Society and F. Jackson's Letter on the Pro-Slavery Character of the Constitution* (New York: AA-SS, 1845), 7.
16. "Change of Opinion Announced" in *Frederick Douglass: Selected Speeches and Writings*, ed. Philip Foner, abridged and adapted by Yuval Taylor (Chicago: Lawrence Hill Books, 1975), 173–74.
17. Ibid., 171.
18. Ibid., 174.
19. Sir William Blackstone, *Commentaries on the Laws of England*, vol. I (Boston: Thomas and E. T. Andrews, 1799), 41.
20. Damon Root, *A Glorious Liberty: Frederick Douglass and the Fight for an Antislavery Constitution* (Potomac Books: University of Nebraska, 2020), 38.
21. Ibid., 39.
22. Douglass, "Change of Opinion Announced," 174.
23. Lysander Spooner, *The Unconstitutionality of Slavery* (Boston: Bela Marsh, 1860), 8.
24. United States v. Fisher, 6 U.S. 358, 390 (1805).
25. Ibid., 59.
26. Root, *A Glorious Liberty*, 53.
27. Theodore Parker, *Life and Correspondence of Theodore Parker*, vol. II, Jon Weiss, ed. (New York: D. Appleton, n.d.), Appendix No. V., 519.
28. He delivered the majority opinion in the infamous 1857 *Dred Scott* case.
29. Douglass, *My Bondage and My Freedom*, 28–29.
30. Philip Foner, ed., *Frederick Douglass: Selected Speeches and Writings*, abridged and adapted by Yuval Taylor (Chicago: Lawrence Hill Books, 1975), 380.

31. Ibid., 383.
32. Ibid., 383–84.
33. Ibid., 384.
34. Ibid.
35. Ibid., 385.
36. Ibid., 386.
37. George S. Schuyler, *Black and Conservative* (New Rochelle, New York: Arlington House, 1966), 2.

Chapter 5: Working the System: Sophistry

1. Arthur Schlesinger Jr.'s prescient book *The Disuniting of America: Reflections on a Multicultural Society* offers a scathing critique of the blatant anti-white racism that masqueraded as Afrocentrism in the early days of Black Studies departments and is worth revisiting for further context.
2. Plato, *Republic*, trans. G. M. A. Grube (Indianapolis: Hackett Publishing Company, 1992), 387b–1.

Chapter 6: Derrick Bell

1. Derrick Bell, *Faces at the Bottom of the Well: The Permanence of Racism* (New York: Basic Books, 2018), 129.
2. The *Wall Street Journal's* Adam Kirsch describes him as the "Godfather" of Critical Race Theory: Adam Kirsch, "The Godfather of Critical Race Theory," *Wall Street Journal*, June 25, 2021, https://www.wsj.com/articles/the-godfather-of-critical-race-theory-11624627522. Bell is described as "intellectual father" in Richard Delgado and Jean Stefancic, *Critical Race Theory: An Introduction*, third edition (New York: New York University Press, 2017), 6.
3. Ibid., 8.
4. Ibid., 177.
5. Derrick Bell, "*Brown v. Board of Education* and the Interest-Convergence Dilemma," *Harvard Law Review* 134, no. 2 (1980): 524, https://harvardlawreview.org/print/no-volume/brown-v-board-of-education-and-the-interest-convergence-dilemma.
6. Bell, *Faces at the Bottom of the Well*, 15.
7. Ibid., 179.
8. Ibid., 181.
9. Ibid., 187–88.

10. Richard Delgado and Jean Stefancic argue that "Unlike traditional civil rights discourse, critical race theory questions the very foundations of the liberal order, including equality theory, legal reasoning, Enlightenment rationalism, and neutral principles of constitutional law." See *Critical Race Theory: An Introduction*, 3.

11. See Paul Edward Gottfried's perceptive response to Walter Block in Walter Block, "To Ban or Not to Ban Critical Race Theory: A Debate," *Chronicles*, September 21, 2021, https://chroniclesmagazine.org/web/to-ban-or-not-to-ban-critical-race-theory-a-debate.

Chapter 7: Ta-Nehisi Coates

1. Ta-Nehisi Coates, *Between the World and Me* (New York: Spiegel & Grau, 2015), 42.

2. David Brooks, "Listening to Ta-Nehisi Coates While White," *New York Times*, July 17, 2015, https://www.nytimes.com/2015/07/17/opinion/listening-to-ta-nehisi-coates-while-white.html.

3. Coates, *Between the World and Me*, 87.

4. Ralph Ellison, "The World and the Jug" in *The Collected Essays of Ralph Ellison*, John F. Callahan, ed. (New York: The Modern Library, 1995), 167.

5. Coates, *Between the World and Me*, 10.

6. Ibid., 17.

7. Ibid., 24.

8. Richard Major, *Cool Pose: The Dilemmas of Black Manhood in America* (New York: Jossey-Bass Inc. Pub, 1992).

9. Coates, *Between the World and Me*, 32–33.

10. Ibid., 39.

11. I'm referring to generational or legacy African Americans. Blacks who were born on American soil prior to the Civil War.

Chapter 8: Ibram X. Kendi

1. Ibram X. Kendi, *Antiracist Baby*, illustrated by Ashley Lukashevsky (New York: Penguin, 2020), 5.

2. Ibram X. Kendi, *How to Be an Antiracist* (New York: One World, 2019), 13.

3. Ibid., 9.

4. Ibid., 19.

5. See "Affinity Groups," KCD, n.d., https://www.kcd.org/about/diversity-equity-and-inclusion/affinity-groups.

6. Kendi, *How to Be an Antiracist*, 62.

7. See Ibram X. Kendi, "Pass an Anti-Racist Constitutional Amendment," Politico, n.d., https://www.politico.com/interactives/2019/how-to-fix-politics -in-america/inequality/pass-an-anti-racist-constitutional-amendment.

8. Luck egalitarians believe that an individual's well-being (material comfort, status, etc.) should be based on the individuals' choices, not on their unchosen circumstances. See Fishkin on luck egalitarians and redistributive justice. John Rawls, best known for his book *A Theory of Justice*, was a very influential political philosopher who died in 2002.

9. Thomas Sowell, *Wealth, Poverty and Politics* (New York: Basic Books, 2016), 98.

10. Kendi, *How to Be an Antiracist*, 16.

11. Ibram X. Kendi (@ibramxk), "Some White Colonizers 'adopted' Black children . . .," Twitter, September 26, 2020, 2:04 p.m., https://twitter.com/ ibramxk/status/1309916696296198146.

Chapter 9: Robin DiAngelo

1. Robin DiAngelo, *White Fragility: Why It's So Hard for White People to Talk about Racism* (Boston: Beacon Press, 2018), 89.

2. Frank Dobbin and Alexandra Kalev, "Why Doesn't Diversity Training Work? The Challenge for Industry and Academia," *Anthropology Now* 10, no. 2 (2018), 48–55, doi.org/10.1080/19428200.2018.1493182.

3. Carolyn Henzi Plaza, Daniel Robotham, and Suzanna Windon, "Diversity Training in the Workplace," PennState Extension, March 10, 2021, https:// extension.psu.edu/diversity-training-in-the-workplace.

4. Alex Lindsey, Eden King, Ashley Membere, and Ho Kwan Cheung, "Two Types of Diversity Training That Really Work," Harvard Business Review, July 28, 2017, https://hbr.org/2017/07/two-types-of-diversity-training-that-really- work; see also Carolyn Henzi Plaza, Daniel Robotham, and Suzanna Windon, "Diversity Training in the Workplace."

5. DiAngelo, *White Fragility*, 7, 9.

6. Ibid., 10.

7. Ibid., 11.

Chapter 10: Oikophobia

1. Roger Scruton, "Education and the Advancement of Ethics and Character," *Journal of Education* 175, no. 2 (1993), 93–98.

2. Ta-Nehisi Coates, *Between the World and Me* (New York: Spiegel & Grau, 2015), 86–87.
3. See Benedict Beckeld's *Western Self-Contempt: Oikophobia in the Decline of Civilizations* (Ithaca: Northern Illinois University Press, 2022).
4. Plato, *Republic*, trans. G. M. A. Grube (Indianapolis: Hackett Publishing Company, 1992), 562e7–563a.
5. Although it's true that Burke is referring to class associations in the quote—specifically to Aristocrats who led the Third Estate, the non-pedantic point seems clear enough: intermediary institutions are important to society.
6. See W. E. B. Du Bois, *The Souls of Black Folk* in *The Norton Anthology of African American Literature* (New York: W. W. Norton & Company, 1997).
7. See the scholarly work of Bradford Wilcox, the director of the National Marriage Project and professor of sociology at the University of Virginia. Especially his co-authored book with Wolfinger, *Soul Mates: Religion, Sex, Love, and Marriage among African Americans and Latinos*.

Chapter 11: Race Conscious Policies: Entitlement, Resentment, Alienation

1. Anthony Abraham Jack, *The Privileged Poor: How Elite Colleges Are Failing Disadvantaged Students* (Cambridge: Harvard University Press, 2019).
2. Ibid., 11.
3. Ibid., 74–75.
4. Ibid., 107–8.

Chapter 12: Identity, Nationalism, and Race

1. Martin Luther King Jr., "Letter from a Birmingham Jail" in *The Norton Anthology of African American Literature* (New York: W. W. Norton & Company, 1997), 1856.
2. David Lampo, *A Fundamental Freedom: Why Republicans, Conservatives, and Libertarians Should Support Gay Rights* (Lanham, Maryland: Roman & Littlefield, 2012), xii.
3. Also see Samuel P. Huntington's *Who Are We: The Challenges to America's National Identity* (New York: Simon & Schuster, 2005); Yoram Hazony's *The Virtue of Nationalism* (New York: Basic Books, 2018); Rich Lowry's *The Case for Nationalism: How It Made Us Powerful, United, and Free* (New York: Broadside Books, 2019); and Samuel Goldman's *After Nationalism: Being*

American in an Age of Division (Philadelphia: University of Pennsylvania Press, 2021).

4. Francis Fukuyama, *Identity: The Demand for Dignity and the Politics of Resentment.* (New York: Farrar, Straus and Giroux, 2018), 18.

5. Ibid., 18.

6. Ibid., 24.

7. Ibid., 26.

8. Ibid., 178.

9. Ibid., 174.

10. Ibid., 115.

11. Ibid., 170.

12. Abraham Lincoln, "Gettysburg Address" in *Lincoln: Speeches and Writings 1859–1865* (New York: Library of America, 1989), 536.

13. Ibid., 224.

14. William M. McClay, *The Mystic Chords of Memory: Reclaiming American History* (Washington, D.C.: The Heritage Foundation, 1996).

15. Dan McCarthy, "The Poisonous Religion of the Ruling Class," The American Mind, May 17, 2019, https://americanmind.org/features/recovering-americanism/the-poisonous-religion-of-the-ruling-class.

16. Yael Tamir, *Why Nationalism* (Princeton, New Jersey: Princeton University Press, 2019), 43–51.

17. Aaron Zitner, "America Pulls Back from Values That Once Defined It, WSJ-NORC Poll Finds," *Wall Street Journal*, March 27, 2023, https://www.wsj.com/articles/americans-pull-back-from-values-that-once-defined-u-s-wsj-norc-poll-finds-df8534cd.

18. Matt Rosenberg, "New Census Data: Income Advantages of Marriage Greatest for Blacks," Wirepoints, July 7, 2022, https://wirepoints.org/new-census-data-marriage-bonus-for-kids-greatest-among-black-families-wirepoints.

19. Esther Larson, "Q&A: Brad Wilcox on the State of Fatherhood in America—and What Can Be Done to Make It Better," Deseret News, June 15, 2023, https://www.deseret.com/2023/6/15/23758334/fathers-day-brad-wilcox-fatherhood-in-america; see Brad Wilcox, *Get Married: Why Americans Must Defy the Elites, Forge Strong Families, and Save Civilization* (Northampton, Massachusetts: Broadside Books, 2024).

Chapter 13: Conclusion: Comfortable Racism

1. Throughout the book, I have addressed my color-blind argument to conservative
    Americans by name as if they are a monolith. They are not. Those conservatives
    who consider themselves social conservatives or paleoconservatives, I would
    imagine, would be especially sympathetic to my overall argument against what
    is called "woke" ideology. But here, too, paleoconservatives aren't a monolith.
    There are meaningful differences, for example, on the issue of race between
    Samuel Francis, Paul Edward Gottfried, and Robert Nisbet.